BAR MITZVAH

TORAH SCROLL, 17th Century
TORAH CASE, France, 1860
Silver, cast and hammered, floral ornamentation.
Courtesy, The Jewish Museum, New York City

For this commandment which I command thee this day, it is not too hard for thee, neither is it far off. It is not in heaven, that thou shouldest say: 'Who shall go up for us to heaven, and bring it unto us, and make us to hear it, that we may do it?' Neither is it beyond the sea, that thou shouldest say: 'Who shall go over the sea for us, and bring it unto us, and make us to hear it, that we may do it?' But the word is very nigh unto thee, in thy mouth, and in thy heart, that thou mayest do it.

See, I have set before thee this day life and good, and death and evil, in that I command thee this day to love the Lord thy God, to walk in His ways, and to keep His commandments and His statutes and His ordinances; then thou shalt live and multiply, and the Lord thy God shall bless thee in the land whither thou goest in to possess it.

Deut. 30:11

TORAH CROWN AND SHIELD, 20th century
Silver, cutout lettering; Tree of Life motif.
By H. David Gumbel, contemporary Israeli silversmith.
Courtesy, American Fund for Israel Institutions.

BAR MITZVAH

ILLUSTRATED

Edited by:

ABRAHAM I. KATSH

EIGHTH EDITION

SHENGOLD PUBLISHERS, INC.

New York City

The publisher wishes to thank those who have given us the material, text and illustrations. We especially thank the Consulate General of Israel, New York, the Israel Government Coins and Medal Corporation, the Lubavitch Youth Organization and Mr. Leon Jolson, New York.

Many photographs by Frank Darmstaedter.

First Edition, May 1955
Second Edition, June 1959
Third Edition, January 1961
Fourth Edition, November 1964
Fifth Edition, April 1968
Sixth Edition, July 1971
Seventh Edition, October 1976
Eighth Edition, November 1982

ISBN 0-88400-048-6

Library of Congress Catalog Card Number: 76-23713

CONTENTS

LIST OF ILLUSTRATIONS

THE BAR MITZVAH SPEECH,
By Moritz Oppenheim, Germany (1800-
1882). Typical home of 19th century
German Jews. The hanging Sabbath lamp
for oil, in the form of a star, became
a significant fixture in the Jewish home
in Western Europe by the 18th century.
Courtesy, Oscar Gruss, New York

INTRODUCTION

This volume seeks to encourage the Jewish boy who has reached the age of *bar mitzvah* (child of precept) to delve further into the spiritual treasures of his people. Jewish observance requires learning and understanding. "An ignorant man," say our sages, "cannot be pious." Jewish holidays have both an ethical and an educational significance. Thus, Passover stresses the concept of human freedom. *Purim* and *Hanukkah* inculcate the ideals of free worship, the concept of *zedakah,* and the right to be different. Through daily and holiday discipline and practice, many Jewish generations have been able to impart to the young the oneness of God and the glory of His teachings — justice, righteousness, morality, and brotherhood.

The house of prayer, the synagogue, has for centuries been a visible expression of Judaism. Before it was created there was no institution on earth, cleansed of all idolatry and impurity, in which all worshipers could take equal part, and which combined within itself the functions of a house of prayer, a house of assembly, and a house of study. Yet Judaism was never limited to the synagogue: the Jewish home, too, has been of supreme significance in perpetuating the faith.

The language of the Bible and of the prayerbook has been a primary bond of unity in time as well as place. With Hebrew one can open the spiritual doors of the Bible, the Mishnah, and all the other literary treasures of our Jewish tradition. With it one can take part today in the literary creativity of modern Israel.

Jewish youth in America will be doubly rewarded by study of the Jewish heritage, for Hebrew language, law, and culture cemented the foundations of American democracy.

It is inevitable that any minority scattered among the nations of the world be subjected to the concepts of their environment. This truth applies to religious as well as to secular culture. The world has often misinterpreted and misrepresented basic Jewish ideas and practices. Only education can help reduce the area of misinterpretation and misrepresentation.

By studying the vast contributions Judaism has made to world civilization, by knowing the wisdom of our great Jewish sages, by mentally traversing the entire range of what we call Torah, every young Jew will find his life permanently enriched.

Bar mitzvah is not a mere celebration of the passage of time in a boy's life. It is a spur to continued study and understanding of his faith and history, a reminder of the injunction in Joshua: "This book of the law shall not depart out of thy mouth, but thou shalt meditate therein day and night, that thou mayest observe to do according to all that is written therein; for then thou shalt make thy ways prosperous, and then thou shalt have good success." Through all the vicissitudes of our history, education has been the compelling factor in Jewish life. It has been excellently expounded in the ethical will of Judah ibn Tibbon, famed scholar of the twelfth century. "My son," he writes, "make your books your companions; let your cases and shelves be your pleasure grounds and gardens. Bask in their paradise, gather their fruit, pluck their roses, take their spices and their myrrh. If your soul be satiate and weary, change from garden to garden, from furrow to furrow, from prospect to prospect. Then will your desire renew itself, and your soul be filled with delight."

In this book we have sought to provide as a stimulant to intensive study, a sampling of the wisdom and ideals of Judaism. The illustrations, mainly of ceremonial objects, have been invoked to add meaning and concreteness to the practices and observances of Judaism.

Ludwig Lewisohn has contributed a message concerning the significance of the *bar mitzvah* ritual. From Cecil Roth comes an essay on the historical development of the *bar mitzvah* celebration, and from Meyer Waxman a conspectus of Jewish history. Hillel Seidman has supplied material on Jewish observances. Shlomo Katz has contributed valuable information and thanks are also due to Moshe Kohn for his helpful assistance. The descriptions of holidays and festivals are by Abraham Burstein.

I wish to express my deepest gratitude to Moshe Sheinbaum, President of Shengold Publishers Inc. for his constant advice and assistance. Without his vision and encouragement the publication of this book would not be possible.

To all our contributors we express our deep gratitude. May their labors in the vineyard of their people prove ever fruitful.

ABRAHAM I. KATSH

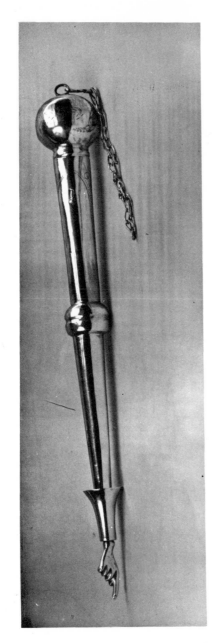

TORAH POINTER, Poland, 19th century
Silver. The pointer ("yad" in Hebrew, meaning hand) is used to follow the text when reading the Torah.
Courtesy, The Jewish Museum, New York City

My son, keep the commandment of thy father,
And forsake not the teaching of thy mother;
Bind them continually upon thy heart,
Tie them about thy neck.
When thou walkest, it shall lead thee,
When thou liest down, it shall watch over thee;
And when thou awakest, it shall talk with thee.
For the commandment is a lamp, and the teaching is light. . . .

Prov. 6: 20-23

14

BAR MITZVAH

Its History and Its Associations

by Cecil Roth

In the traditional Jewish scheme, there were three great festive occasions in a boy's life. There was the eighth day after his birth, when he was introduced into the Covenant of Abraham. There was the day when he was first initiated to study, being taken to synagogue, blessed by the rabbi, and given honey to lick from a slate on which letters of the Hebrew alphabet were written, as a token that the TORAH should be sweet to his mouth all the days of his life. And there was the day when he was first considered legally bound to fulfill the obligations of Jewish law and practice, and could be regarded as a BAR MITZVAH, a "child of precepts."

The precise age at which this stage of a child's life should begin was at one time a little uncertain. Girls mature earlier than boys, and it was generally agreed that a girl reached this point when she had completed her twelfth year. Some authorities were of the opinion that from this point of view boys, *too,* were to be regarded as adults at the same age. But clearly, this is in most cases too early, both physically and mentally. Moreover, one of the most popular of Jewish classics, which was familiar to every Jew, the *Pirke Aboth,* or Ethics of the Fathers, gave its authority to the later point of departure: "At five a child is brought to the Bible, at ten to the Mishnah, at thirteen to Commandments." This was generally accepted in due course. When he had completed a full thirteen years of his life, when he was thirteen years and one day old; on the day *after* his thirteenth birthday, that is — a boy became BAR MITZVAH. Up to that time, it was proper to provide him with moral guidance, to give him instruction, to take him to synagogue, to introduce him little by little into the practice of Jewish observance. From now on, these were obligatory on him. Moreover, they were his responsibility, not his parents'. Hitherto his father had been answerable for his guidance and conduct — the child could not be blamed for any shortcoming. But by now, his moral sense should be sufficiently developed, and he was expected to know and appreciate the difference between right and wrong. In this respect too, therefore, he entered into a new stage of his life.

Judaism comprised a very large number of practices and traditions, which embraced every period of life and every season of the year. Many were the MITZVOT, the obligatory religious practices, which were henceforth incumbent on the Jewish boy. But all did not necessarily recur constantly, from day to day; they were bound up with special occasions, or with special feasts, or with special seasons. But there were a few MITZVOT which constantly recurred, daily or almost daily; and the first time when a boy performed one of these in public in this new stage of his life came to be regarded, very naturally, as an occasion for special celebration. There were two such MITZVOT above all which became associated with the BAR MITZVAH ceremonies. One was the placing on the head and binding round the arm of the TEFILLIN, the phylacteries, during the recital of the morning prayer (except on the Sabbath); there are parts of the world where even now this is the central feature of the BAR MITZVAH celebration. The other was the exercise of the coveted privilege of the Jew, of being summoned to participate in the reading of the Torah in the presence of the congregation and reciting the sublime benediction, thanking God "Who has chosen us from among all nations and given us His Law."

At one time, and indeed in some places even today, this ceremony too would take place very often on a weekday, a Monday or a Thursday, when also readings from the Pentateuchal scroll formed part of the service. It was doubtlessly a proud occasion for him and his parents when he went up to the reading-desk, wearing his TEFILLIN formally for the first time, amid the congratulations of the congregation, and chanted the time-honored formula. In those days, to be sure, the synagogue was not much less attended on a week-day than it was on a Sabbath, and the ceremony thus occasioned received much the same degree of general participation. Later on, however, it became customary to transfer it for the sake of greater publicity to the following Sabbath, when the TEFILLIN were not worn. Thus, so far as the public celebration goes, the essential part of the BAR MITZVAH ceremony came to be the formality of being summoned to the reading of the Torah.

Originally, every person who was summoned to the Torah was expected to be able to read his own portion, and did so, the regular officiant reciting the passage in an undertone for his guidance should it be necessary. Later on, it was found more practical for the officiant to read aloud, and the person summoned to the Torah to read in an undertone, however well qualified he might be; for otherwise those less learned would be put publicly to shame. The older practice was however preserved, or revived, in favor of the BAR MITZVAH; he, at least, having been summoned to the reading of the Torah, actually chanted his portion in the time-honored fashion, unless there were good reason why he should not do so. This too is not universal — in some Sephardi communities, for example, the practice is unknown. But in general it became the characteristic feature of the BAR MITZVAH ceremony. Sometimes indeed the BAR MITZVAH boy would show his ability by reading the entire portion of the Law for that week.

TORAH CASE by Ludwig Yehuda Wolpert, Jerusalem. Presented to President Harry S. Truman by Chaim Weizmann, first President of the State of Israel, 1949.
Courtesy, the Honorable Harry S. Truman, Kansas City, Missouri.

Before we leave this aspect, there are two further points connected with the ceremony that should be mentioned. It has been pointed out above that until the son reached his religious majority the father was regarded as responsible for his moral conduct. Hence it became customary for the father to recite, after his son had concluded the blessing over the Law, his own special benediction: "Blessed be He Who hath relieved me of the responsibility for this child" — a thanksgiving for having been privileged to complete this all-important stage in his son's education. The recital of this formula was considered an integral part of the celebration, hardly less than the boy's own participation in the service. Again, having now attained his majority from the religious point of view, the boy could henceforth be counted one of the *minyan* of ten persons, whose presence constitutes a proper quorum for the recital of public prayers with full formality. This fact too was regarded as being an important feature of the celebration — so much so that among the Sephardim the usual term for becoming BAR MITZVAH in many lands is "to enter into *minyan*."

How far back does the institution of the BAR MITZVAH go? It was formerly held that it became a fixed rite only as late as the fourteenth century, in Germany. But it is demonstrable that it goes back before, and perhaps long before, this period. In the *Masseketh Sopherim*, probably composed in the fifth or sixth century in Palestine, we are told how it was formerly the practice in Jerusalem for a man to introduce his child by degrees into the observance of the religious precepts; but after he had attained twelve years of age and had fasted for the first time on the Day of Atonement he was taken to all the elders and scholars, who blessed him and prayed for his well-being; and then they all went in procession with him to the greatest of the scholars in the place, before whom he did reverence and supplicated his blessing.

Here, obviously, we have a description, perhaps somewhat idealized, of a full-fledged ritual observance. Another source informs us how the great Babylonian scholar of post-talmudic times, Jehudai, head of the Academy of Sura from 757 to 761, rose to his feet when his son was called to the Torah for the first time in the synagogue and recited the benediction: "Blessed be He Who has relieved me of the responsibility for this child." Once again, we seem to have here, in this factual anecdote from the eighth century, a picture of a well-rounded ceremonial, basically the same as that which applies at the present time.

Later on in the Middle Ages, however, and especially from the fourteenth century onwards in Germany, the celebration attained a greater significance, and the rabbinical writings of this period begin to discuss and to elucidate minor points connected with it; for example, who should recite the father's blessing in the case of an orphan. The public reading from the Torah was rightly considered only symbolic. A bright child, if he had really received the elements of a full Jewish training, should have gone by now beyond the biblical text: he should have been introduced at least into the full flood of Jewish lore and literature — that is, to the study of the Talmud. In order to demonstrate his prowess in this discipline, it became customary for him to give a public or semi-public discourse; not a speech of thanks, or an exhortation, but as it were a lecture revolving about some point of rabbinical learning. Thus yet another element, the discourse, entered into the traditional BAR MITZVAH ceremony. This would take place most often not in the synagogue but at home, before an audience of appreciative greybeards, as the climax of a banquet which was given to celebrate the occasion. The Polish talmudists indeed held that this learned *hors d'oeuvre* transformed the function into a *seudat mitzvah,* an obligatory festivity. Moreover, this being the first occasion

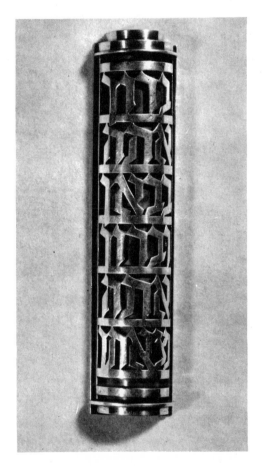

The *mezuzah* (from the Hebrew word meaning "doorpost") is a small wood, metal, or plastic receptacle, attached to the upper right post of a house or any room that is occupied. It contains a portion with two sections of the Pentateuch — Deuteronomy 6:4-9 and 11:13-21. These express the Jewish faith and treat of God's love and commandments. There may be a small upper opening displaying the word "Shaddai" — "Almighty." The *mezuzah* is used as the result of the biblical injunction: "And thou shalt write them upon the doorposts of thy house, and upon thy gates."

MEZUZAH, silver with cut-out lettering, by Ludwig Yehuda Wolpert, Jerusalem

when the duty of reciting grace was legally incumbent upon him (the casuunists discussed the hypothetical case of a boy who completed his thirteenth year after he had eaten, but before grace was recited!) the hero of the occasion would have the honor of leading in the chant of that lovely, elaborate recital.

Thus in the course of time the BAR MITZVAH became one of the great festive occasions in the cycle of Jewish life, second only to the marriage. This feature has attained its greatest development during the past hundred years or so in western Europe and America, but to some extent it was known long before this. There are casual mentions of festive celebrations associated with the BAR MITZVAH well back in the Middle Ages, but they were probably on a small scale. By the seventeenth century, they had increased to such a degree that they began to constitute something of an abuse, and the communities tried to restrict the degree of expenditure and ostentation. Even in Poland, where the institution of the BAR MITZVAH never attained such importance as it did elsewhere (probably because learning was here considered to be of paramount importance not bound up with any specific age or period), the Council of the Four Lands decreed in 1659 that no more than ten strangers might be invited to a BAR MITZVAH feast — these, however, always to include one poor man, who should be able to share in the rejoicing. German sumptuary laws (as they were termed) in restriction of extravagance and ostentation, were more detailed; and here in the eighteenth century some communities solemnly enacted a regulation forbidding the BAR MITZVAH boy to wear a wig on this occasion, in the adult fashion of that time. (The picturesque current story, that he was obliged to wear one, his head being shaved as part of the preliminary ceremonial, is based on an unfortunate misreading of the sources.) In Ancona, in the gloomy twilight day of ghetto life in the eighteenth century, when the Jews lived in perpetual dread of exciting antagonism, it was forbidden outright by the *pragmatica* of 1766 to give a festive meal on the occasion of a BAR MITZVAH to any outside the immediate family, though coffee and sweetmeats might be served to those who called at the house to offer their congratulations.

In more recent times, various new elements began to be added to the traditional BAR MITZVAH celebrations. In the Italian ghetto, it was customary to celebrate every conceivable occasion in private or family life by composing, and frequently publishing, Hebrew verses and poems. From the first part of the eighteenth century at the latest, and probably a good time earlier, such poems began to be produced in honor of the boys who had to become BAR MITZVAH: at Leghorn, for example, it seems to have become an accepted institution by about 1720 at the latest. From Italy, the usage spread to Holland, and thence to England. One of the persons who seems to have especially favored compositions of this type was the erudite schoolmaster, Hyman Hurwitz, friend and in some measure collaborator of Samuel Taylor Coleridge, one of whose productions in this sphere was printed on silk for distribution to honored guests. It was accompanied by the text of the speech made in English by the hero of the occasion.

This introduces us to another new feature. The discourse formerly given by the BAR MITZVAH boy had been intended to demonstrate that he had received a proper training in rabbinic studies. Now, in western countries, this gave way increasingly to a formal speech, of a moralizing tendency, mainly comprising a profession of religious fervency and gratitude to the parents for their training. In our own day, large numbers of specimen addresses of this type have been published, especially in America, adapted to all possible occasions (including the special requirements of twins who were BAR MITZVAH together!).

As in the course of recent generations the institution of a sermon during the Sabbath morning service became general in western countries (as distinct from the old-time talmudic discourse held later in the day), it became natural for this to be linked with the BAR MITZVAH ceremony, should one take place on that day; and the BAR MITZVAH sermon has now become a regular institution. In the second half of the nineteenth century, the rabbi of the Spanish and Portuguese Synagogue in London, Haham Benjamin Artom, in order presumably to compensate for the relatively small eclat of the ceremony in his community (where the practice of chanting the scriptural passage by the BAR MITZVAH boy was as yet unknown), composed a special prayer and profession of faith for him to recite after he ascended the reading-desk. This has since been adopted by many other communities, Ashkenazi as well as Sephardi, and has by now attained some of the dignity of tradition. On the other hand, in some environments the recital of a single portion of the Torah has come to be considered an inadequate demonstration of ability, and the chanting of the additional prophetical reading, the *Haftorah*, has become very common. In a way, this is a retrogression, for (especially in Sephardi and Italian communities) the chanting of the *Haftorah* on an ordinary Sabbath was regarded as a special prerogative of children, well below BAR MITZVAH age. Leone Modena of Venice recounts how he first performed this function at the age of two-and-a half; and the ancient Bevis Marks Synagogue in London preserves an eighteenth century mahogany stool, in three steps, to bring small children up to the level of the reading desk when they took part in the service in this or some similar fashion.

A few communities, on the other hand, to ensure that the BAR MITZVAH should not remain an empty formality, and that preparation for the synagogue ritual should not be the sum total of a boy's religious training, have instituted examinations in the elements of Jewish knowledge as preliminary to the ceremony, and issue certificates testifying that the candidate has satisfactorily acquitted himself.

In some parts of the Jewish world, different ceremonials, sometimes highly picturesque, were observed. In the famous Sephardi Synagogue of Amsterdam, for example, the ceremony took place not on Sabbath morning, but in the afternoon, during the *Minhah* service; and the BAR MITZVAH was escorted to the reading desk by two sponsors (*padrinhos*). In Morocco, in former days, the boy was expected to have studied profoundly one of the tractates of the Talmud — generally, in fact, he learned it by heart — and it was only after he had passed a test in this that he was considered ripe for his religious majority. On Wednesday, a banquet would be given to which the rabbis and scholars were invited. On the following morning, service would be held at the boy's home, not in the synagogue, and a venerable rabbi would ceremonially place the TEFILLIN on his arm, and his father those on his head, while the assembled guests chanted a special hymn. This being a Thursday, a section from the Torah was recited, and he would be "called up" to it, though here it was not usual for him to read his section. At the end of the service, if he were capable, he would deliver a discourse. The points he raised would be discussed by the rabbis present, and afterwards the boy would be blessed aloud by the whole assembly. He then went around the congregation with his TEFILLIN bag, into which all would drop silver coins, which he then presented as a gift to his teacher. This in fact was the BAR MITZVAH ceremony; but it was rounded off on the following Sabbath, when he attended service in synagogue and recited the prophetical portion or *Haftorah*.

Among the Marranos of Spain and Portugal who from the fifteenth century onwards preserved some sort of Jewish tradition in the secrecy of their homes notwithstanding all the persecutions of the Inquisition, the conception of the BAR MITZVAH seems to have received a remarkable development. Obviously, the unhappy crypto-Jews were faced with a difficult problem in connection with the education of their children. If they brought them up in the traditions of Judaism from the beginning, their innocent talk might betray the whole family to death. If they waited until they reached manhood, it might be too late: and cases were known of some unhappy youths and maidens who actually betrayed their own parents to the authorities when the subject of their true religion was at last broached. The obvious compromise was the age between childhood and manhood, the threshold of adult life. It appears that the Marranos chose for this purpose the old institution of BAR MITZVAH. When a child reached the age of thirteen years he was not confirmed in, but introduced to, the rites, customs, and beliefs of traditional Judaism. This as it seems was the method through which the Jewish heritage was kept secretly alive among the Marranos for three hundred years.

As we have seen, the BAR MITZVAH ceremony has known many changes and gone through many stages since it first emerged in Jewish religious life so many centuries ago. But the basic idea has remained. It is not a question of the public display of a child's vocal powers, but something finer and more splendid. On this day, the boy who has entered fully into the religious heritage of his people has for the first time the privilege of leading the congregation in a prayer, of reciting in their presence a passage from the Torah given at Sinai, of being counted one of the *minyan,* and of returning thanks to God for the proud gift of being a Jew.

TEFILLIN CASES (PHYLACTERIES), Poland, 19th century
Silver, engraved
Courtesy, The Jewish Museum, New York City

TEFILLIN

And I will betroth thee unto me forever:
Yea, I will betroth thee unto me in righteousness, and in judgment,
And in loving kindness, and in mercy:
I will even betroth thee unto me in faithfulness:
And thou shalt know the Lord.

Hosea 2: 21,22

Tefillin, or phylacteries, are donned every morning, except on Sabbaths and festivals, by observant Jews, beginning with *bar mitzvah* age. They are worn throughout the morning prayers. The word *tefillin* is a late plural of the Hebrew word for prayer, *tefillah.*

The *tefillin* are two cubical leather containers with attached leather thongs. They hold parchments with four biblical passages, expressing four basic Jewish precepts — the law of *tefillin,* recognition of God's kingship, the unity of the Creator, and the exodus from Egypt.

23

One of the *tefillin* is worn on the forehead, the other on the left upper arm. When the arm is bound, one recites: "Blessed be Thou, O Lord our God, King of the universe, Who hast sanctified us with Thy commandments, and hast commanded us to wear *tefillin*." This thong is wound seven times about the forearm. When the head phylactery is put on, with its thongs hanging loosely behind head and shoulders, the benediction ends . . . "and commanded us to observe the precept of *tefillin*."

The arm thong is then wound three times about the middle finger, with the formula: "And I will betroth thee unto me forever; yea, I will betroth thee unto me in righteousness, and in judgment and in lovingkindness, and in mercy. I will even betroth thee unto me in faithfulness; and thou shalt know the Lord" — the Lord's declaration to the congregation of Israel. The rest of the thong is then wound about the hand, to resemble the letter *shin*. This, with the letter *yad*, formed by the thong against the heart, and *dalet*, on the head, forms the word *Shaddai* — one of the Hebrew names of God.

The *tefillin* must rest against the skin. They must be handled in reverence, and be donned and doffed while the worshiper is standing. They are removed in reverse — the loops are slipped from the middle finger, then the head thong is taken off, and finally that on the arm.

The *tefillin* remind us of our liberation from Egypt; of the requirement that we accept God's commandments in love; of the need for providing the young with a religious education; of the behest to avoid wrongdoing and to think holy thoughts; and of our hopes for the redemption of Zion, containing among others the commandment: "Thou shalt love the Lord thy God with all thine heart, with all thy soul, and with all thy might." The *tefillin* are worn on the head, the seat of thought, and on the arm, the instrument of action, opposite the heart, the seat of feeling — thus teaching that all our thoughts, feelings, and actions must conform to the will of God. Since the Sabbaths and festivals are themselves signs or symbols to the Jew, *tefillin* are not required on those days.

Prayer is a universal phenomenon that few men fail to live by. The Jews have afternoon and evening congregational prayers also, as well as additional services for the holidays. The Bible itself is filled with supplications, which Israel never failed to employ even in the darkest of hours.

The Hebrew word *tefillah* comes from a root meaning self-examination or an appeal for justice, and does not imply begging or pleading or wishing. Our Hebrew prayers are always couched in the plural and not in the singular.

שמע ישראל ה׳ אלהינו ה׳ אחד

ארבע פרשיות התפילין

וידבר יהוה אל משה לאמר קדש לי כל בכור פטר כל רחם בבני ישראל באדם ובבהמה
לי הוא ויאמר משה אל העם זכור את היום הזה אשר יצאתם ממצרים מבית עבדים כי
בחזק יד הוציא יהוה אתכם מזה ולא יאכל חמץ היום אתם יצאים בחדש האביב והיה כי יביאך
יהוה אל ארץ הכנעני והחתי והאמרי והחוי והיבוסי אשר נשבע לאבתיך לתת לך ארץ זבת
חלב ודבש ועבדת את העבדה הזאת בחדש הזה שבעת ימים תאכל מצת וביום השביעי
חג ליהוה מצות יאכל את שבעת הימים ולא יראה לך חמץ ולא יראה לך שאר בכל גבלך
והגדת לבנך ביום ההוא לאמר בעבור זה עשה יהוה לי בצאתי ממצרים והיה לך לאות על ידך
ולזכרון בין עיניך למען תהיה תורת יהוה בפיך כי ביד חזקה הוצאך יהוה ממצרים ושמרת את
החקה הזאת למועדה מימים ימימה   והיה כי יבאך יהוה אל ארץ הכנעני כאשר
נשבע לך ולאבתיך ונתנה לך והעברת כל פטר רחם ליהוה וכל פטר שגר בהמה אשר יהיה לך
הזכרים ליהוה וכל פטר חמר תפדה בשה ואם לא תפדה וערפתו וכל בכור אדם בבניך תפדה
והיה כי ישאלך בנך מחר לאמר מה זאת ואמרת אליו בחזק יד הוציאנו יהוה ממצרים מבית
עבדים ויהי כי הקשה פרעה לשלחנו ויהרג יהוה כל בכור בארץ מצרים מבכר אדם ועד
בכור בהמה על כן אני זבח ליהוה כל פטר רחם הזכרים וכל בכור בני אפדה והיה לאות על
ידכה ולטוטפת בין עיניך כי בחזק יד הוציאנו יהוה ממצרים
שמע ישראל יהוה אלהינו יהוה אחד ואהבת את יהוה אלהיך בכל לבבך ובכל נפשך ובכל
מאדך והיו הדברים האלה אשר אנכי מצוך היום על לבבך ושננתם לבניך ודברת בם בשבתך
בביתך ובלכתך בדרך ובשכבך ובקומך וקשרתם לאות על ידך והיו לטטפת בין עיניך וכתבתם
על מזזות ביתך ובשעריך   והיה אם שמע תשמעו אל מצותי אשר אנכי מצוה אתכם
היום לאהבה את יהוה אלהיכם ולעבדו בכל לבבכם ובכל נפשכם ונתתי מטר ארצכם בעתו
יורה ומלקוש ואספת דגנך ותירשך ויצהרך ונתתי עשב בשדך לבהמתך ואכלת ושבעת
השמרו לכם פן יפתה לבבכם וסרתם ועבדתם אלהים אחרים והשתחויתם להם וחרה אף יהוה
בכם ועצר את השמים ולא יהיה מטר והאדמה לא תתן את יבולה ואבדתם מהרה מעל
הארץ הטבה אשר יהוה נתן לכם ושמתם את דברי אלה על לבבכם ועל נפשכם וקשרתם אתם
לאות על ידכם והיו לטוטפת בין עיניכם ולמדתם אתם את בניכם לדבר בם בשבתך בביתך
ובלכתך בדרך ובשכבך ובקומך וכתבתם על מזוזות ביתך ובשעריך למען ירבו ימיכם וימי
בניכם על האדמה אשר נשבע יהוה לאבתיכם לתת להם כימי השמים על הארץ

Four sections of the Torah are placed within the tefillin that declare the absolute unity of God and His deliverance of the Israelites from Egyptian bondage.

"LEARNING TO DON THE TEFILLIN" by S.
Bender, " . . . and thou shalt bind them for a sign
upon thine hand . . . " (Deut. 6:8).
Courtesy, Library of The Jewish Theological
Seminary of America, New York City.

"PUTTING ON THE TEFILLIN" woodcut by Ilya Schor, New York City, 1951 "
. . . and they shall be for frontlets between thine eyes . . . " (Deut. 6:8)

MY DEAR BOY

So the time has come when you are going to be called to the Torah. Your parents are happy and proud; you yourself are probably a little nervous. And it is indeed a very deep and very moving day and hour for you, and not only for you and for your parents and teachers but for all Israel. Because your being called to the Torah means that you are from now on a Bar Mitzvah, a son of the divine command, which in turn means that you are now committing yourself *of your own free will* to obey the divine command. And that means that the Community of Israel is increased by one more member. And in all ages but especially in this age Israel needs men, *needs you,* not only for the sake of Israel but for the sake of the whole world.

Now the sign of your commitment and dedication to the Community of Israel is being called to the Torah and pronouncing the blessings over the Torah. And these blessings, these *berakhot,* are strange eternal sayings which we must all say when we are called to say them, with profound devotion and perfect understanding, because they express and sum up the entire history and the entire character of the Jewish people and so of every Jew and so of yourself as a Jew.

The first blessing tells us that at Mount Sinai God sanctified us above all other peoples by giving us His Law. And young as you are, you must already know that that is true. The world around you will show you that that is true. In many parts of the world there are cold wars and fiery wars, and lovingkindness among men seems farther off than ever. But God's Law which was given to us from Sinai bids us and all men love each other and cultivate peace. And the Jewish people has now for many, many centuries obeyed that Law of God and has sought in all days and in all seasons to be at peace, to practice peace and to spread peace abroad over the earth. And this is especially true of wise and learned Jews, such as your parents and your teachers hope that you will become, according to the saying: *Talmide haakhamim marbim shalom b'-olam* "The disciples of the sages will spread peace throughout the earth." And if you need further proof of this you can recall, or ask your parents and teachers to recall for you, that Jews have never been the persecutors but even until this very day the persecuted.

Now when the Torah portion has been read you are called to pronounce another blessing. And that other blessing contains an even deeper historic truth or, rather, two of the truths whereby we live. One truth is that the Torah which the Eternal has given us is a true Torah. He who obeys it — as your parents and teachers hope you will obey it — is at peace and creates peace. And the other truth is that God has placed eternal life in our midst. And if you will remember that all the other nations among whom we lived in ancient days have disappeared and that we and we alone, though so few and so persecuted from age to age, from Haman to Hitler, have survived and are here and have founded and built in this age the State of Israel, you will understand that this second blessing too is not just a string of pious words but the statement of a truth, of a fact, which none can deny. Lastly you will be *Maftir*, that is, you will intone the *Haftarah* or prophetic portion of the Sabbath on which as a Bar Mitzvah you enter the community of Israel. And again you will see that the prophets of Israel spoke and prophecied truly, as when Samuel told the people of Israel what would be then fate if they sought to be like all the peoples: as when Isaiah described the people of Israel as the suffering servant of mankind; as when Amos foretold the reconquest by the means of peace of Eretz Israel and the ingathering of the exiles from the four corners of the earth. But now comes the most serious question, my dear boy, that must be asked of you. When the great day of your being called to the Torah and becoming a Bar Mitzvah and entering the community of Israel — when that solemn and beautiful and rightly festive day is over, what then? What will you do then as a member of the Holy Community?

The day, I beg you to remember, is the day of a beginning only. You commitment is for always, is for life. Israel needs you. It needs you not today only. It needs you always; it needs your devotion, your learning, your good deeds. For the spirit of the Divine does indeed rest upon Israel, as a great sage has said, but it can continue to rest upon Israel only in so far as it rests upon every Israelite — in so far at is rests upon you.

And another sage has told us that Israel has survived and rendered true the saying concerning the eternal life that is in its midst, by virtue of its *unity*. But what is the meaning of that unity? It means that every Jew is and remains united to Israel by the study, the devotion, the dedication of his total existence, and every lad who becomes a Bar Mitzvah, by pledging himself to the cause, the life, the survival of his people.

It is in this way that Israel has survived. It is in this way that Israel has endured the onslaughts of the ages and has born aloft the torch of God's Law and righteousness in an ever darker world. Every Jew, by what he is, bears witness to God and to God's Law and is in his own person and by the intensity of his Jewish existence, a protest against the heathenism and the evil that fill the world. But it must be in very truth on the part of every Jew — and so on your part — an entire and intense Jewish existence: an existence of ever widening Jewish knowledge. of ever deepening alliance with Synagogue and community, of never-tiring devotion to the cause of the State of Israel. What we need, what the world needs, is *whole* Jews, entire Jews, integrated Jews, life-long Jews. And such Jews will be happy Jews, Jews and human beings at one with themselves, at peace with themselves — knowing who and what they are and what, as Jews, is their function and destiny in history.

May you be such a Jew! May Israel be enriched by you! And may you be sustained and elevated by Israel!

LUDWIG LEWISOHN

"THE TALMUDIST" Oil by Max Weber
Courtesy, The Jewish Museum, New York City ▶

THE TEN COMMANDMENTS

I am the Lord thy God, who brought thee out of the land of Egypt, out of the house of bondage.

Thou shalt have no other gods before Me. Thou shalt not make unto thee a graven image, nor any manner of likeness, of anything that is in heaven above, or that is in the earth beneath, or that is in the water under the earth; thou shalt not bow down unto them, nor serve them; for I the Lord thy God am a jealous God, visiting the iniquity of the fathers upon the children unto the third and fourth generation of them that hate Me; and showing mercy unto the thousandth generation of them that love Me and keep My commandments.

Thou shalt not take the name of the Lord thy God in vain; for the Lord will not hold him guiltless that taketh His name in vain.

Remember the sabbath day, to keep it holy. Six days shalt thou labor, and do all thy work; but the seventh day is a sabbath unto the Lord thy God, in it thou shalt not do any manner of work, thou, nor thy son, nor thy daughter, nor thy man-servant, nor thy maid-servant, nor thy cattle, nor thy stranger that is within thy gates; for in six days the Lord made heaven and earth, the sea, and all that in them is, and rested on the seventh day; wherefore the Lord blessed the Sabbath day, and hallowed it.

Honour thy father and thy mother, that thy days may be long upon the land which the Lord thy God giveth thee.

Thou shalt not murder.

Thou shalt not commit adultery.

Thou shalt not steal.

Thou shalt not bear false witness against thy neighbor.

Thou shalt not covet thy neighbor's house; thou shalt not covet thy neighbor's wife, nor his man-servant, nor his maid-servant, nor his ox, nor his ass, nor anything that is thy neighbor's.

Exod. 20: 2-14

The Bar Mitzvah Celebration
For The Children Of
The Fallen Heroes In Israel

For many Israeli youths, the joy of Bar Mitzvah is tinged sadness because their fathers have fallen in defense of their country. Since the Six-Day War in 1967, members of the Lubavitch movement have brought joy and understanding to them through a special program of religious instruction at their village of Kfar Chabad.

These Bar Mitzvah boys, from all parts of Israel, spend a week or more at the Lubavitch village where they participate in the life style of Kfar Chabad, including attending classes, from which they gain insight into the values of Chassidism. They celebrate their Bar Mitzvah at a large ceremony attended by relatives and distinguished guests headed by the President of the State of Israel, the Prime Minister and chief officers of the Israel Defense Forces, as well as thousands of well-wishers from throughout the country who come to honor the sons of the nation's fallen heroes.

This Bar Mitzvah program is a special part of an outreach movement run by the Chassidim of Lubavitch for the familes of Israel's fallen heroes.

Ephraim Katzir, President of the State of Israel, welcomes a group of Bar Mitzvah boys to his residence. To his left are Mrs. Shifra Golombowitz, who directs the Lubavitch efforts on behalf of the families of Israel's fallen heroes. Mrs. Katzir is seated next to her. Also seated behind President Katzir are members of the Lubavitch movement, who devote a great deal of time to this program.
Courtesy, Friends of the Families of the Fallen Heroes.

Prime Minister Yitzhak Rabin speaks to the Bar Mitzvah boys at the celebration. "You are our future," he told this group, "as you enter adulthood and become full-fledged members of the House of Israel."
Courtesy, Friends of the Families of the Fallen Heroes.

A group of Bar Mitzvah boys and their mothers pose with President and Mrs. Katzir, Mrs. Golombowitz and leading members of the Lubavitch movement in Israel.
Courtesy, Friends of the Families of the Fallen Heroes.

Since the liberation of the Western Wall by the Israel Defense Forces during the Six-Day War in 1967, thousands of boys from Israel and many other countries have observed their Bar Mitzvah at the Wall.
Courtesy, Consulate General of Israel, New York.

Carrying a Torah in an intricate Sephardic case, a Bar Mitzvah boy comes to the Wall accompanied by his family and friends. He will read from the Torah in front of the Wall and then be joined by other members of his family for a small reception.
Courtesy, Consulate General of Israel, New York.

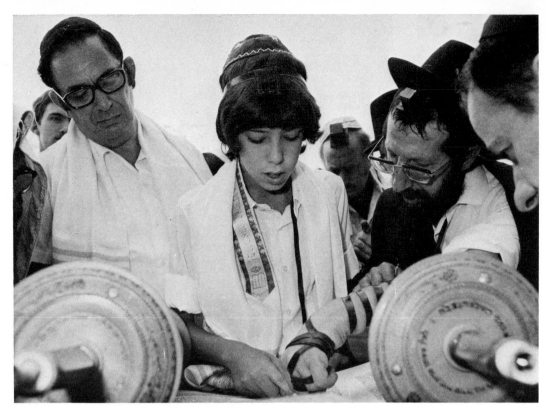

A proud father looks on as his son reads from the Torah at the Western
Wall on his Bar Mitzvah day.
Courtesy, Consulate General of Israel, New York.

Family and friends dancing around a Bar Mitzvah boy near the Western
Wall in Jerusalem.
Courtesy, Consulate General of Israel, New York.

The Holocaust and the Will to Live

by

Abraham I. Katsh

In the 19th century Victor Hugo wrote, "War will be dead, the scaffold will be dead, hatred will be dead, frontiers will be dead, royalty will be dead, dogmas will be dead, man will begin to live." But here we are in the 20th century. War is not dead, the scaffold is not dead, dogmas are not dead, and man does not know how to live. Verily this is a killing century, of terror, destruction and devastation, marred by moral cynicism. The mind of man, trained by generations in science and education, is shockingly applying the results to the perfection of weapons of death. Just because man's capacity for destruction has become almost unlimited, the need becomes greater to rekindle man's awareness of a higher purpose in the human destiny.

Our own generation has witnessed the unthinkable horror of the Holocaust and the systematic extermination of six million Jews, men, women and children.

The Holocaust visited on the Jews was different from all the earlier massacres in Jewish history because of its conscious and explicit planning, its systematic execution, and the absence of any emotional element in the remorselessly applied decision to *everyone,* but *everyone,* to the exclusion of any possibility that someone might escape or survive. There was no chance for survival!

The terror afflicted on all its victims, in disregard of the Commandment "Thou shalt not kill" — nor take life without proper trial, nor kill the defenseless, nor harm the innocent — was in this case so unprecedented in its violence that it is difficult to grasp how even an insane or half-sane fanatic would find it in himself not only to conceive such a plan, but to decree that "Thou shalt kill" millions and an entire nation without evoking the immediate horrified reaction from the world: "Why, you must be out of your mind!"

How, we wonder, did Hitler obtain the consent and cooperation of his closest associates, the compliance of the mass of executioners and the resigned acceptance of the very many who did not care or who were unwilling to get into trouble, but who all knew

Almost a year before the outbreak of World War II, the quiet of a November night was broken when the synagogues of Germany were destroyed in a act of violence and desecration that prefigured the horror of the Holocaust. Known as "Chrystallnacht" ("The Night of the Breaking Glass"), the event took its name from the sound of synagogue windows shattering throughout the country. Ironically, the passage of the United Nations resolution equating Zionism with racism took place on the 38th anniversary of Chrystallnacht.

fully, partially or dimly, what was going on, and chose not to rebel or to ask questions.

A vast literature has been written on the Holocaust, but unfortunately, most of the world, even in our own time, shies away from reading it. Death is always tragic, but when death by murder is multiplied by the dimension of 6 million in five years, counting only the Jewish victims, the deed becomes so enormous, so inconceivable that a new term had to be coined for it: *Genocide.*

When Judeo-Christian tradition was undermined in the Holocaust, the resurgence of primitive paganism in modern guise was made possible. As for the victims, one is not certain who was the real hero — the soldier who marched into battle with a song on his lips, completely equipped with all modern arms, or the isolated Jew, living under tragic conditions in the ghettos, imbued only with a zeal for life and an indomitable faith at a time when there was no hope. This zeal and struggle to resist when resistance was impossible evinced the noblest expression of the will to live.

To live is one thing, to will to live is another. To live is an assignment to which we are conscripted. To actually will to live is instinct and choice. To will to live with a firmness of purpose, with courage, with a taste for life, even in the face of pain, frustration, and adversity, is something of a resounding vote of open-eyed confidence in the act of being. It is an enlightened exercise of preference for life over death.

Nazi soldiers smile as though on a holiday outing, while a pious Jew in "tallith" and "tephillin" is forced to stand near the bodies of slaughtered Jews. The Nazis frequently humiliated their Jewish victims and forced them to break religious laws in an effort to break their spirit.

This struggle to resist tyranny and to retain dignity and integrity as human beings, at a time when the conscience of the world seemed mute, evidenced the noblest expression of the will to live, with faith in the Almighty that justice will ultimately prevail.

The Jewish people were a small, weak, impoverished minority, caught between two powerful majorities (the local population and the invading enemy), both equally terrifying and both aiming to destroy them. One common point united those enemies, the conquerors and the conquered; the determination to wipe out the Jew completely. History cannot recall such a predicament, as the Jews found themselves as a minority in Europe, helpless, despised and ostracized, vulnerable to attack on all sides, and lacking in any potential for self-defense.

No foreign enemy ever head from German lips what Jews heard constantly: "The last bullet will be for a Jew." With all the doors closed to him and without weapons of defense, there was no escape from German hands. In contrast to this hopeless situation of Jews, the world saw how a Western army equipped with the best and most modern weapons in the world faced Hitler, and took six years of war, with the concentration of all forces and strategic intelligence, to finally overcome the Nazis.

The will to live in such a horrible tragic situation, unparalleled in history, is clearly described in a detailed diary of the Warsaw Ghetto written in Hebrew by Chaim A. Kaplan,* which I discovered and translated from the Hebrew and edited with

* *The Warsaw Hebrew Diary of Chaim A. Kaplan,* translated and edited by Abraham I. Katsh, Collier Books, New York, 1973.

notes. Kaplan lived in Warsaw with dignity even under the indignities of the Nazis, and he wrote in the ghetto a daily chronicle that could be called a pragmatic poem, for, while it deplored the evils about him, also cheered the existence of life and toasted the life of existence.

Kaplan writes: "In the eyes of the conquerors we are outside of the category of human beings. This is the Nazi ideology, and its followers, both common soldiers and officers, are turning it into a living reality. Their wickedness reaches the heights of human cruelty.

On January 16, 1942, he wrote: "The whole nation is sinking in a sea of horror and cruelty . . . I do not know whether anyone else is recording the daily events. The conditions of life which surround us are not conducive to such literary labors . . . Anyone who keeps such a record endangers his life, but this doesn't alarm me. I sense within me the magnitude of this hour and my responsibility to it. I have an inner awareness that I am fulfilling a national obligation . . . My words are not rewritten, momentary reflexes shape them. Perhaps their value lies in this . . . My record will serve as source material for the future historian."

The will to live gave Kaplan the stamina to record the days of misery for history; he was sure that there would be a tomorrow.

And now *our* today is *his* tomorrow. Kaplan no longer breathes, but the pulse of his passion for life still beats in the diary bequeathed to us. Written in flawless Hebrew, Kaplan's diary is an imposing document of 1500 pages, covering the years between 1939 to the end of 1942. Each paragraph was composed with a sense of danger, lest it be discovered by the German invaders. Each paragraph communicates the urgency of providing an accurate record of ghetto living and the will to live.

"Some of my friends and acquaintances who know the secret of my diary urge me, in their despair, to stop writing. 'Why? For what purpose? Will you live to see it published? Will these words of yours reach the ears of future generations? How?' . . . And yet in spite of it all I refuse to listen to them. I feel that continuing this diary to the very end of my physical and spiritual strength is a historical mission which must not be abandoned. My mind is still clear, my need to record unstilled, though it is now five days since any real food has passed my lips. Therefore I will not silence my diary!"

On another day, Kaplan writes: "If anyone in the democratic lands is attempting to write a book on the nature of Nazism, I know without seeing it that the author will fail. Descriptive literary accounts cannot suffice to clarify and emphasize its real quality. And, moreover, no writer among the Gentiles is qualified for this task. Even a Jewish writer who lives the life of his people, who feels their disgrace and suffers their agony, cannot find a true path here. Only one who has examined the various nuances of its administrative and legal tactics in relation to the Jews, unequaled in hard-heartedness, sadistic cruelty, warped sensibility, petrification of human feeling, and stupidity — only such a writer, if he is a man of sensitivity, and if his pen flows, might be able to give a true description of this pathological phenomenon called Nazism."

On April 26, 1942, Kaplan writes: "The Nazi terror does not stop. The ghetto dwellers fear for their lives. When they go to bed they are doubtful of seeing the light of day; when they go to work or to attend to their 'affairs' they are doubtful of returning home; on their way home, they wonder whether they will arrive safely.

"The Nazis employ three kinds of terror. The first is the terror of shooting. This terror threatens every Jew who commits the very slightest misdeed. The Jew is punished on the spot: without warning, without inquiry or investigation, without trial or verdict. The Jew is not considered a human being and therefore, they think it better to save all the trouble involved in 'administration.' Here the penalty follows not the crime, but the mere suspicion.

"The second type of terror is beatings. They attack Jews who are walking along minding their own business, and in the sight of thousands of passers-by beat them up brutally. If a Nazi crooks his finger at a Jew from a distance, that gesture is a command to approach him immediately and 'willingly.' The intention is of course to give the Jew a merciless beating.

"The third type of terror is humiliation, which is a matter of course followed by physical violence, too. The moans of the tortured one become merged with the Homeric laughter of the torturer and of his colleagues who witness the incident.

"Terror stalks up and down the entire ghetto in all its ferocity. Humiliations, beatings, shootings occur by the dozen every day. No private person can possibly check or count them. I shall, therefore, limit ,myself to what I personally saw only today."

"The Jewish people have always lived in material and spiritual straits. Our enemies have always engulfed us to destroy us. Yet Jewish creativity never ceased throughout all the days of our exile. Moreover we created more in the lands of the diaspora than we did in our homeland. This is the strength of eternal Judaism, that it continues to spin the fibre of our lives even in hiding.

"The fact that we have hardly any suicides is worthy of special emphasis. Say what you wish, this will of ours to live in the midst of terrible calamity is the outward manifestation of a certain power whose quality has not yet been examined. It is a wondrous, superlative power with which only the most established communities among our people have been blessed.

"We are left naked, but as long as this secret power is still within us we do not give up hope. And the strength of this power lies in the indigenous nature of Polish Jewry, which is rooted in our eternal tradition that commands us to live." Polish Jewry says, together with our poet laureate Chaim Nachman Bialik:

"One Spark is hidden in the stronghold of my heart,
One little spark, but it is all mine;
I borrowed it from no one, nor did I steal it
For it is of me, and within me."

Father Neimuller once remarked, when, alas, it was all too late:

"First it was the Jew, but I wasn't a Jew so I didn't react —
Then it was the worker, but I wasn't a worker so I didn't react —
Then it was the Catholic, but I wasn't a Catholic so I didn't react —
Then it was me, but I was too late ...."

The martyrs of the ghettos restored the image of God in man, for they did not go to be slaughtered as sheep. Rather, it was humanity as a whole which, in its silence and indifference, behaved like lambs.

A Talmudic statement reads as follow:

"The earth borrows from the sky, and the sky from the earth;
The day borrows from the night, and the night from the day;
The moon borrows from the stars, and the stars from the moon.
In all God's creation, one creature borrows from the other, and Nature's
harmony remains unbroken. Man alone borrows from His brother, only
to be oppressed and despoiled in the process."

(Exod. Raba)

Instead of being attuned to the inability to remain comfortable and at ease in the presence of those who are in trouble and in pain, man has become attuned to complacency. To fight terror means to remember the past and say to yourself: Remember, it could have been the reverse, *they* here and *we* there. Remember not to forget.

The Jews are a people of memory, and this monumental sculpture, entitled "Uprising," reminds us of the valor of the defenders of the Warsaw Ghetto. The inscription is from Ezekiel: "Come, O breath, from the four winds and breathe upon these slain, that they may live." The work is by sculptor Nathan Rapoport and was presented by Mr. Leon Jolson. It is located at Yad Vashem, Martyrs' and Heroes' Remembrance Authority, in Jerusalem.

Soviet Jewry: Journey To Freedom

During the late 1800s and early 1900s, so many Russian Jews immigrated to the United States that it is easy to forget the millions who remained behind. Yet they did, and today there are about 3 million Jews in the Soviet Union.

For a time after the 1917 revolution, the character of some Jewish communities in various districts remained distinct and individual Jews gained prominence in the new regime. But their power could not help their people and before long it became obvious that Jews were perceived as increasingly "cosmopolitan" elements in Soviet society, aliens in a homogeneous culture.

The life of the Jews during the long Stalin era was harsh and cruel in many respects. In the last years before Stalin's death, many Jewish writers and leaders were purged and disappeared, never to be heard from again.

Under the Soviet regime, Jews were required to assimilate, yet the spirit of Judaism remained alive. When Golda Meir come to Moscow as the first ambassador of the new Jewish State, she was mobbed in the streets by Jews who wanted to touch someone from Eretz Israel. Eventually, it was not enough for Soviet Jews to only touch someone who had been in Israel; many of them wanted to get and live there themselves. After the stunning Israeli victory in the Six-Day War of 1967, Soviet Jewry began agitating for exit visas that would enable them to begin lives of freedom in Israel and other democratic nations.

The Soviet government has tried domestic countermeasures of harassment and imprisonment of dissidents and has intensified an international program to discredit Israel, Jews and Zionism. But the example of courage and principle displayed by the Jewish activists in the Soviet Union has galvanized the Jewish communities of the free world, and, together, world Jewry is working for the release of their brethren.

Message From Jews In The U. S. S. R.
To The Second World Conference On Soviet Jewry
Held In Brussels, Belgium In February, 1976

(Signed by more than 100 Soviet Jewish activists from major Soviet cities, including: Vladimir PRESTIN, Beniamin FAIN, Vladimir LAZARIS, Ida NUDEL, Viktor BRAILOVSKY, Yevgeny ABEZGAUZ, Aba TARATUTA, Yakov SHVARTSMAN, Ilya ZLOBINSKY, Tsilia LEVINZON, Mikhail MAGER)

"We greet you from far-away Russia. Five years ago you gathered in Brussels to support the fight of Soviet Jews to mass emigration to Israel. We

Medal issued in commemoration of the Second World Conference of Jewish Communities on Soviet Jewry held in Brussels, Belgium, February 1976.
Courtesy, Israel Goverment Coins and Medal Corporation.

remember today with profound gratitude that your efforts have helped over 100,000 Soviet Jews to be re-united with their historic homeland. We hope that your present World Conference will play an equally important role in the fate of Soviet Jewry.

"This hope is strengthened by our recognition that the Jews are a people with a single destiny and a single fate. We are also aware, however, that we exist as a people only as long as we choose to be one. Each day we recreate ourselves as a nation, because each day we make the decision to be one people and to remain Jews. Every generation has confronted the necessity of making this choice. It was this choice that preserved our people throughout the centuries. Today the "silent" generation of Soviet Jews must make this choice as well. On each individual Soviet Jew will depend whether world Jewry tomorrow will number 15 million persons or whether it will lose another 2.5 million of its compatriots. Such a loss can be compared only with the death of 6 million of our brethren in the Nazi death camps.

"The present generation of Soviet Jews has never before faced the necessity of making a deliberate national choice. For these Jews grew to maturity assimilated into Soviet society, but not of their own decision. This had been the choice of their fathers, who saw in the assimilation forced upon them the road towards social and cultural progress, towards an exit from the pale of settlement and towards the realization of the age-old Jewish dream of universal justice and peace. Motivated by that lofty hope, they consented to the conditions forced upon them and permitted their national language, their schools, their publishing houses and other Jewish cultural traditions and facilities to be taken away from them and from their children.

"This choice was a fatal error. We assert this not because, feeling ourselves to be Jews again, we wish to force our choice upon others. Rather, our words are confirmed by sixty years of Soviet Jewish history: the revival of anti-Semitism and discrimination which, for the past thirty years, have been the official norm of Soviet ideology and Soviet policy. Their degradation, the absence of national rights that is their lot, is reflected in their social and cultural backwardness. Our fathers were ready to forget they were Jews in the hope that others would also forget. But their Jewishness was neither forgotten nor forgiven and, 30 years later, they were "reminded" of their Jewish ancestors. But their contribution to Soviet science and culture and the blood that they shed on the front lines during the Great Patriotic War — these were forgotten.

"Can we really hope that the next generation would not be also threatened by more attacks against "cosmopolitans," by another "doctors plot," by more murders of Jewish intellectuals by another Leningrad trial, by the trial and sentencing of more Prisoners of Conscience? What protects them from even worse national tragedies? This is why, in full responsibility, we assert that assimilation is not and cannot become the solution to the Jewish question in the U. S. S. R. Having renounced their former national traditions, the assimilated Soviet Jews have not created any new ones. The values borrowed from others have brought only sorrow, degradation and shame. The road towards assimilation, forced upon us, has brought our generation to a dead end.

"This is why the situation of Soviet Jewry has become so drastic today, demanding an equally drastic solution. Soviet Jewry is being driven toward such a solution by increasing discrimination, growing anti-Semitism and the ever-stronger realization that while Soviet Jews have no future in the U. S. S. R., they do have a future elsewhere. It is understandable that the possibility of emigration to Israel has played and continues to play a great role in the awakening of Jewish consciousness in assimilated Soviet Jews. However, the mere existence of this possibility cannot by itself overcome the natural doubts and fears that do exist. Today, with assimilated Soviet Jewry on the threshold of emigration, its waverings and hesitations — caused by the lack of national roots — are to be expected, making the choice to leave more difficult and resulting in a certain slow-down in the tempo of Aliya.

"But this slow-down, caused in large part by the campaign of intimidation and repression against us, does not signify by any means that the great reservoir of Jews planning to emigrate to Israel has become exhausted. On the contrary, today there are not scores but hundreds of thousands prepared to make the great choice: the choice between gradual disappearance into an alien culture or national revival.

"It is only national revival that guarantees both mass emigration to Israel and the very survival of Soviet Jewry.

"Therefore we consider that the main task at hand is the unity and strengthening of all efforts aimed at protecting and supporting the mass movement of Jews to Israel, along with a many-sided effort to promote the great national revival of Soviet Jewry. At present all our modest resources are devoted to those problems. We appeal to you to help us in this great cause.

"Fate has turned us into 'refuseniks' — Jews who are refused the right to emigrate. Fate has doomed us to long and painful waiting, to deprivation and to danger. But we are grateful for it because it has permitted us to be with our people. Today, as great historic changes slowly ripen to fruition, we are grateful for the fate that has permitted us to understand the tragedy of our people and its needs and to serve in its preservation and its revival.

"If we are fated to give our lives to the cause, we are ready."

Moscow, February 1976.

The Spirituality
of the State of Israel

by

Abraham I. Katsh

The beginning of Jewish colonization and settlement in early Israel was linked not only with a passion for acquisition of land, but for the fulfillment of ideals. The people who rebelled against exilic life wanted solid ground under their feet. In this, they were much like other nations, but the desire that stirred them was derived from the noblest spiritual inspirations. These dictated the paths to be followed and the forms to be adopted in the idealistic life of the early pioneers. It is difficult to conceive the heroism of those settlers, unless it is realized that it had its origin in the great values which sustained Judaism through many generations and which now drove these new heroes to establish a land where the spirit of Israel could again blossom and bear fruit.

It is a logical and natural development which transformed Israel, even before the birth of the State, into a melting pot of spiritual life with all its magnificent manifestations. The *Halutz* movement which founded the kibbutzim; the daily labor, with all the obstacles and trials of time and reality that accompanied it; the stubborn, unyielding struggle in defense of the land — all these were results of those idealistic forces which moved the people and directed their growth.

To the Jew, the land, whether barren or desolate, was always good and beautiful, a land with "streams and springs and lakes... a land whose rocks are iron and from whose hills you can mine copper... a land flowing with milk and honey." At all ceremonies, from the day of birth to the day of his death, the words Eretz Yisrael were part of the Jewish ceremony.

The refined spirituality of Israel is, therefore, not a chance occurrence. On the contrary, it constitutes the natural path of development. The creation of the State was an expression of the greatness of Israel's culture and spirit. This is a unique phenomenon. The great cultural and spiritual treasures which distinguish many nations do not impose themselves and their authority on the life of their respective lands, as is the case in Israel.

No matter what the issue, and no matter how many adherents clamor for the final authority of civil, and not religious, law, few see in Israel a state estranged from the traditional ways of Judaism. Although much of Israel's Jewry no longer follows the dictates of Orthodoxy, it does not uproot traditional Judaism. Rather, it tries to adapt traditional meaning and form to present-day concepts. Hence, the varied impressions one gathers in Israel on the Sabbath and the holidays. One can find their observance in all the details and punctilios dictated in the *Shulhan Arukh,* as well as what amounts, from the orthodox point of view, to "profanation" of the holidays. But even those who do not observe the Sabbath and holidays preserve the beauty of these days, and give them a character not to be found anywhere else in the world.

One is always aware of the operation of spiritual factors to a degree quite unexpected in view of the country's size and population. Israel is rich in cultural life, art exhibits and unusual collections of the spiritual and the creative, which arouse exceptionally wide interest and response. The general atmosphere is so filled with cultural values that it seems to put all other issues in secondary position.

JERUSALEM — THE KNESSET STATE MEDAL. (Obverse) The Knesset building which crowns one of the lovely western hills of Jerusalem. (Reverse) Stylized panorama of reunited Jerusalem with outstanding landmarks arranged in a free composition.
Courtesy, Israel Government Coins and Medal Corporation.

This is not only an aspect of the unquestionable high mentality of the people. What is noteworthy is the permanence and continuity of this phenomenon. There are no occasional high peaks of cultural activity followed by periods of dormancy or decline. The cultural spirit is a fixed and permanent background of the State of Israel. It is not something apart. It is an integral phase of the private life of every individual.

I do not know of any other country in which commercial firms engage in the spread of classical literature. Morning and evening newspapers and their publishers all distribute the Hebrew classics, from the Bible, Talmud, Maimonides, and Midrashim, to modern literature, encyclopedias and scientific works. The distribution of these volumes is usually in the form of prizes to subscribers, but it is based on the profit motive. The large scale of this continuous distribution activity indicates a demand on the part of a public which is proud to own such volumes. Nowhere else do newspapers engage in distributing literary works of this caliber and on such a scale. In other lands, apparently there is little demand for such books. In Israel, such business pays.

Book publishers, too, keep expanding their activities. Books — originals and translations, science, research, art, classical works — are published at the rate of about one a day. In their beauty, quality of printing and technical excellence, these can match the best books published anywhere. Israeli publishing houses base their business on the purchasing power of the readers and not on governmental or private support. And the readers, comprising the entire population, have not disappointed them. The reading public is out of proportion to that in any other country, and is apparently at home in all areas of Jewish and universal culture. The concept of the "People of the Book" thus designates not only the Jews of the past, but the Jews of the present. Books symbolize the character of the new Israel.

Another example of the spirituality of the country is the attitude of Israel Defense Forces. In its numerous branches, beginning with the youth battalions, the *Nahal* (pioneering-fighting youth), and ending with the regular units, especially the Frontier Guards, one finds not youth shaped and formed by the Army, but an Army which gains its idealistic character from the nation's youth.

Israel is the only country in the world where, twice a month, on a Saturday evening, the President, a Supreme Court Justice, the Minister of Education, a President of a University, and several other scholars, convene to discuss the teachings of the Bible. How pleasant and how invigorating to see politicians, statesmen, scholars and religious leaders of the atomic age sit together at a Melave Malka,* and study the true prophetic meaning of the word "Shalom."

Various factors were responsible for the redemption of our culture as a result of the emergence of the State of Israel. One was the revival of the ancient Hebrew language. With the reclaiming of the soil of ancient Israel, the language of the prophets became alive again.

Israel has shown that the tongue of the prophets was never dead to the Jew. Throughout the vicissitudes in life, the Jews wrote official correspondence in Hebrew and continued to study our great Hebrew literary treasures. When Jews of different countries and cultures met, Hebrew was the written medium through which they could understand each other, even though it was a kind of literary Hebrew, composed of phrases and quotations from the Hebrew Bible or Hebrew literature. Hebrew was used during all ceremonies and rites, from the moment the Jew was born until his death.

Thus, it was natural that the Hebrew language, the tongue of the prophets, became the national language of Israel, for it is Hebrew that represented our title-deed to the soil

* Held at the conclusion of the Sabbath to say farewell to the holiness of the day and usher in the new week.

TEL AVIV JUBILEE MEDAL. (Obverse) To the left of the Shield of David is the passage from Job 8:7, "Though thy beginning was small, yet thy latter end shall greatly increase," in Hebrew. (Reverse) Tel Aviv depicted schematically with its houses and streets. In large Hebrew lettering is "Tel Aviv" with the Hebrew years "5669-5719" alongside an olive branch. Courtesy, Israel Government Coins and Medal Corporation.

MASADA STATE MEDAL. The Rock of Masada in relief. At its base, the remnants of the camps of the besieging legions of Rome are distinctly recognizable. Above the Rock, there is again an arrangement of Hebrew characters, the letters now spelling out — 'We shall remain free men!', and, again, the phrase appears in English also in a half-circle on the lower rim.
Courtesy, Israel Government Coins and Medal Corporation.

of Israel. A knowledge of Hebrew helped redeem our souls and restore the roots of our dignity.

The poet, David Shimoni, beautifully expresses this idea:

"Oh tongue of my muse, Thou Hebrew of old
We are one in the blood, indivisible twin
Worlds long forgotten in both of us spin
Ancient stock and abandoned of kin
Mysterious echoes of ages untold."

The national Hebrew poet, Chaim Nachman Bialik, prophetically stated: "The land of Israel left us a legacy in the Hebrew language: One little Book. Who knows, perhaps this Book may ultimately restore the land to us."

Israel is more than an outpost of the West, as some have described it. It is a bold experiment in human and geographic rehabilitation, a pilot plant in social engineering. It has become a visual aid of the Bible. It is unique in so many ways, and some of its innovations hold such promise for the West, that it requires interpretation for those unfamiliar with what is transpiring in this small but dynamic land.

Israel represents the righting of age-old wrongs of unbearable misery and long humiliation and the constancy of the people's faith and hope. To deny Israel's right to live its corporate life as a nation is to deny its right to exist and its importance to contribute and share in the welfare of nations. To invite the Jews to live as Jews, and to be faithful to "Judaism" without fulfilling their existence as a people with a land, is sheer hypocrisy. All Israeli life is affected by the memories of Auschwitz and Dachau. The history of 2000 years of pogroms, massacres, slaughter, murder and burning is deeply rooted in the minds

47

and hearts of all citizens. Those who appeal to Israel to relinquish this claim actually invite it to relinquish its identity, and to commit corporate suicide — or to have themselves massacred once more. It is an appeal so outrageously immoral that Israel can accept it neither from its enemies nor from its "friends." For Jewish history has taught that everything horrible is possible when it relates to the Jew, regardless of how incomprehensibly outrageous and horrifying the mind can invent.

How does Israel contribute to the welfare of those of us who live in the Diaspora? First, in a single lifetime we have passed from a world in which the existence of a free Israel seemed inconceivable to a world that seems inconceivable without its existence. Once excluded from every major achievement, we are today an essential factor in the union of nations. We are counted in the Minyan.

Within this short time, the Magen David, for centuries a symbol of degradation and martyrdom, now has become Israel's flag. It is a symbol of creativity and glory — a symbol of joy and respectability.

Israel is challenging the world to become aware that the thousands of years of Jewish martyrdom were not in vain and that the utterances of "Ani Maamin" (I believe), or "Shema Yisrael," whether by the martyrs in Rome, in Spain, or during the Holocaust, had a prophetic meaning and have become true.

Israel is making the world realize that the Jewish people throughout ages have made a vital contribution to the sum total of world civilization, and that the world has benefitted immensely from this contribution.

Israel is restoring the Jew in the Diaspora to his historic address, where he can live not by sufferance, but by joy.

For centuries, the world tried to define Judaism as a religion... as an atheistic system... as a communist philosophy...any term that benefitted the detractor. Now the world must listen to Israel for the definition of the Jew. For our people to live in a world where our own culture is represented among all cultures is indeed a historic novelty.

How beautiful and how meaningful it is to live in a great democracy like the United States and, at the same time, feel that, as a result of Israel, our Jewish culture, too, is represented without any need for apology. How exciting it is to feel that we, too, are represented in the exhibitions of books, in the exhibitions of stamps, in the halls of learning, in the jet planes, in the collections of coins, in the challenges for the spiritual enrichment of mankind.

How beautiful it is to watch how the State of Israel has forced the American press and publishers to take cognizance of Jewish culture and Jewish civilization. Let us not forget that more books dealing with Judaism have appeared in the past three decades than in the preceding three centuries of Jewish life in America.

Israel means that the Jews, the only people in the world to belong to an ancient people whose lineage has never been severed, are no longer servants to humanity but contributors to civilization.

Israel means that the Jew, degraded and vilified for centuries as Shylock and Fagin, now stands boldly and nobly as a member of an old and honorable nation with an abundant venerable culture.

Israel means that, for the first time in two thousand years, the Jew has a place under the sun where the term majority includes our people.

How beautiful to be master of our own destiny! How beautiful to be able to stand erect and be counted! How beautiful is to be a member of the minyan.

"MOSES" by Don Benaron, New York City, 1954, Mahogany sculpture, derived from the Hebrew letter "Shin", Made for Ira Haupt Chapel of Temple Beth Miriam, Elberon, New Jersey

THIRTEEN PRINCIPLES

1. I believe with perfect faith that the Creator, blessed be His name, is the Author and Guide of everything that has been created, and that He alone has made, does make, and will make all things.

2. I believe with perfect faith that the Creator, blessed be His name, is a Unity, and that there is no unity in any manner like unto His, and that he alone is our God, Who was, is, and will be.

3. I believe with perfect faith that the Creator, blessed be His name, is not a body, and that He is free from all the accidents of matter, and that He has not any form whatsoever.

4. I believe with perfect faith that the Creator, blessed be His name, is the first and the last.

5. I believe with perfect faith that to the Creator, blessed be His name, and to Him alone, it is right to pray, and that it is not right to pray to any being besides Him.

6. I believe with perfect faith that all the words of the prophets are true.

7. I believe with perfect faith that the prophecy of Moses our teacher, peace be unto him, was true, and that he was the chief of the prophets, both of those that preceded and of those that followed him.

OF THE JEWISH FAITH

8. I believe with perfect faith that the whole Law, now in our possession, is the same that was given to Moses our teacher, peace be unto him.

9. I believe with perfect faith that this Law will not be changed, and that there will never be any other law from the Creator, blessed be His name.

10. I believe with perfect faith that the Creator, blessed be His name, knows every deed of the children of men, and all their thoughts; as it is said, it is He that fashioneth the hearts of them all, that giveth heed to all their deeds.

11. I believe with perfect faith that the Creator, blessed be His name, rewards those that keep His commandments, and punishes those that transgress them.

12. I believe with perfect faith in the coming of the Messiah, and, though he tarry, I will wait daily for his coming.

13. I believe with perfect faith that there will be a resurrection of the dead at the time when it shall please the Creator, blessed be His name; and exalted be the remembrance of Him for ever and ever.

Maimonides

"STUDYING THE TALMUD" Oil by Isidor Kaufman, Austria (1853-1921).
Courtesy, Oscar Gruss, New York City

Nachmanides' Letter To His Son

"Hear, my son, the instruction of thy father, and forsake not the teaching of thy mother." Make it your custom to speak calmly to all men and at all times, and you will be saved from anger, which is an evil attribute causing men to sin

. . . . And when you are saved from anger, your heart will acquire the attribute of humility, which is the best among all ways of goodness: — as it is written, "The reward of humility is fear of the Lord." . . . And if you constantly accustom yourself to the way of humility, and act modestly before all men, fearing God and fearing iniquity, then the *Shekhinah* (Divine Presence) with its glorious resplendence, will rest upon you, and you will live in the life of the world to come.

And now, my son, know and understand, that he who in his pride glorifies himself above all creatures, rebels against the very kingdom of heaven . . . . For before God all are equal. In His anger He humbles those who are proud; and if He so desires, He elevates those who have been humbled. Therefore make yourself humble, and the Omnipresent will uplift you.

Hence let me expound to you why you should act humbly, and walk in that path at all times. Let all your words be spoken in restraint. Bend your head and turn your eyes downward toward the earth, while your heart seeks the heavens. Do not stare into a man's face when you address him. And in your eyes may every man be greater than yourself. If he is wise or wealthy, it is your duty to give him honor. But if he be poor, and you be wealthier and wiser, ponder in your heart that you may have more guilt than he, and that he may be more righteous than you. Think that when he commits a sin, he does so through inadvertence, whereas when you sin you do so with forethought. And at all times imagine that you stand before the Holy One, blessed is He, With His Glory Over You, "for the whole earth is full of His glory." . . . And be heedful ever to read the Torah, so that you may render it into actuality. When you rise from the book, fathom what you have studied, to know whether there be aught in it which you can transmute to reality. Analyze your deeds both morning and evening, and thereby all your days will be marked by penitence. When you pray, rid your heart of all worldly matters. Prepare your soul before the Omnipresent, blessed is He, and purify your thoughts. Consider your speech ere it leave your mouth. Act in this manner all the days of your life, in every matter, and you will not commit iniquity. Thereby your words and your deeds and your thoughts will be upright. Your *prayers* will be clear, pure and innocent, devoted and acceptable to the Omnipresent, blessed is He. As it is written: "Thou wilt direct their heart; Thou wilt cause Thine ear to attend."

My son, strive to know yourself, to know and understand your Judaism, your wonderful, unique history, the inseparable connection of your people with the patriarchs and the prophets. You will then realize that you are part of the religious-national covenant of Israel, of the Holy Ark, an exemplar of the very covering of the Ark! You will be proud of your historic people and happy in your sublime faith.

We expect that your life and conduct shall ever proclaim the eternal values which Israel received from Sinai, that by your daily religious exercises, by your prayers and *tefillin*, by your observance of the Sabbath and the festivals, of *kashrut* and all the sanctifying, elevating commandments of our holy Torah, you will re-echo the divine voice within the innermost recesses of your heart and mind. Let your life and conduct echo the divine command issued on Mount Sinai: "Honor thy father and thy mother, in order that thy days may be long!" You will honor them, indeed, by becoming a true son of Israel and a loyal and useful citizen of the country of your birth or adoption, reflecting honor upon those whose life is completely wrapped up in yours, upon those to whom you are dearer than life itself.

My son, the future of your great, martyred people lies in your hands! Resolve now firmly to hold fast to Israel's inalienable divine heritage, to work for the spiritual and material welfare of your historic people, and for the land divinely promised to Abraham, Isaac, and Jacob. May you become a source of blessing to yourself, to those dear to you, and to the entire house of Israel, Amen!

From a Message by

DR. ISAAC HALEVI HERZOG,

Chief Rabbi of Israel (1888-1959)

"Command the children of Israel, that they bring unto thee pure olive oil beaten for the light, to cause a lamp, to burn continually."

Lev. 24:2-3

ETERNAL LIGHT by William B. Meyers, Newark, New Jersey. A modern design, based on a new concept of the burning bush..

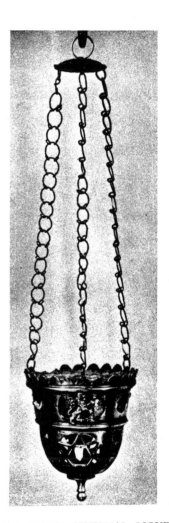

NER TAMID (ETERNAL LIGHT), Italy, 17th Century, brass. Courtesy, The Jewish Museum, New York City.

I AM A HEBREW

I will continue to hold my banner aloft. I find myself born — ay, born — into a people and a religion. The preservation of my people must be for a purpose, for God does nothing without a purpose. His reasons are unfathomable to me, but on my own reason I place little dependence; test it where I will it fails me. The simple, the ultimate in every direction is sealed to me. It is as difficult to understand matter as mind. The course of the planets are no harder to explain than the growth of a blade of grass. Therefore am I willing to remain a link in the great chain. What has been preserved for four thousand years was not saved that I should overthrow it. My people have survived the prehistoric paganism, the Babylonian polytheism, the aesthetic Hellenism, the sagacious Romanism, at once the blandishments and persecutions of the Church; and it will survive the modern dilettantism and the current materialism, holding aloft the traditional Jewish ideals inflexibly until the world shall become capable of recognizing their worth.

CYRUS ADLER (1863-1940)

PRAYER BOOK, Italy, mid-19th century silver with metallic embroidery on velvet, set with garnets and pearls. Courtesy, The Jewish Museum, New York City

THE AUTHORIZED DAILY PRAYER BOOK
Based mainly on Amram Gaon's (9th century) *siddur,* first compilation of a full Hebrew liturgy. To Jews, the *siddur* has been both the gate to communion with God and a spiritual bond for Jews in every place and period.

BAR MITZVAH BOY MAKES A SPEECH
by Sholom Aleichem

It was a glorious, festive day at the home of Nahum Rabinowitz. It was bar mitzvah day.

There were many hands busy in arranging and preparing for the big event, all under the close supervision of Grandma Minde. For the occasion she had put on her holiday best — including an expensive headdress — and she ruled her dominion with an iron hand, like a mighty ruler whose bidding everyone stands ready to perform and whom no one dares disobey. None moved a finger without her approval. She made all the decisions and settled all the problems: who was to be invited to the party and where each was to be seated; the courses on the menu, and when each was to be served.

She managed to get into arguments with everybody. Not one escaped a tongue lashing. Even the hero of the occasion — the bar mitzvah boy — did not get off without a good scolding. He must behave like a man among men today, not bite his fingernails, not laugh, and not make others laugh. In short, he was not to carry on like a silly child, but mind his manners.

In addition to the many guests invited to the Rabinowitzes right after the services, all the kinfolk were there: Aunt Hannah and her children, Uncle Pini and his brood, and all the rest of the near ones and dear ones. Needless to say, among those present was the teacher, Reb Moshe David, dressed in his broad Sabbath *caftan* and his frayed and faded plush hat.

The big moment came — time for the big test. The bar mitzvah boy had to climb up on the table and begin his speech. Reb Moshe David, the teacher, suddenly came to life and went into action. His back straightened; his black, bushy eyebrows arched; and his piercing eyes were fixed on his pupil's face. His thumb swept through the air, up and then down, like a baton in the hand of an orchestra conductor, and the boy had the signal to start his speech.

As the terrified lad climbed on the table, looked down on the heads of the seated guests, and saw their eyes fixed on him, waiting for him to speak, he almost collapsed from fright. His eyes blurred, his knees buckled, his tongue became dry and stuck to his palate, and he was completely confused. He felt as though he were standing on thin ice; any minute it would crumble beneath him, and he and everyone present go tumbling into the deep.

But his confusion lasted only a moment. No sooner did he catch his teacher's eyes and the movement of his thumb, than he pulled himself together. Once he started speaking, all his fear and stage fright vanished. His mind cleared and his voice grew firmer and louder. Now he felt sure of himself every step of the way, as though he were marching across a sturdy bridge of iron. He kept warming up to his speech from moment to moment, until he felt such a warmth through his body, such a delightful sweetness, the like of which he had never felt before.

All the time the bar mitzvah boy stood on the table following the movements of his teacher's thumb, he was engrossed in his speech; nevertheless he did not fail to notice his audience. He looked them over from time to time, and saw their eyes and the expressions on their faces.

Yes, he glanced at everyone seated about the table; he noticed their every gesture, caught their every expression, even the faces of his chums. Oh, that gang! So they thought they would confuse him and get him to laugh by making faces at him! Now they too sat motionless, their mouths open in amazement, silent and admiring.

Yes, the bar mitzvah boy saw everything. Now his eyes rested on the beaming face of his father. He could see that there was no happier man in the world than father at this moment. His posture was proud and erect, his head held high. His lips followed every movement of his son's lips, his face was aglow with joy, and his eyes roamed the whole assemblage, now resting on his brother Pini, now on Reb Moshe David, and now on the bar mitzvah boy's mother.

And the mother, little Hayah Esther? She stood humbly and reverently to one side, together with the other women, wrapped in her silk Sabbath shawl, all aflutter, sighing softly every so often, cracking all her knuckles at one time, and two tears, like shining pearls, rolled down her cheeks and sparkled by the light of the sun on her blissful face.

(from the Hebrew by Moshe M. Kohn)

"ADORATION OF THE MOON", oil painting by Max Weber
Collection of Whitney Museum of American Art, New York City

Tishri (30 days)

Marheshvan (29 or 30 days)
(Heshvan)

Kislev (29 or 30 days)

ON THE JEWISH CALENDAR

The Jewish calendar and the calendar generally employed differ in many respects. The years and months are not the same, nor do they coincide in arrangement. But these are not the only distinctions between them. For every day in the Jewish year is given a sacred character, not alone the Sabbath and the important holidays. Each day is sanctified by prayers and prescribed conduct. Each fast or festival has its special significance, to remind us of our past, to be sure, but also to revive some moral principle and improve every Jew's character and disposition. Character is bettered by moral instruction; disposition is altered by creating feelings of joy even in the midst of oppression, by reassuring us all that God and the good will ultimately triumph.

The calendar of the Jews dates back to the biblical account of Creation. It celebrates a divine event. It covers the entire known history of man's consciously developing life on earth, while never permitting him to forget that a Divine Intelligence was and is responsible for all life and the universe.

The Jewish calendar is based on changes of the moon and not of the sun. There is a new moon every twenty-nine or thirty days. In olden days, before calculations of changes in the heavens were made mathematically exact, witnesses would report to the chief court in Jerusalem that they had seen the moon emerging; and that day would be pronounced *Rosh Hodesh,* or the New Moon. Through lofty bonfires and torches the news was spread throughout the land of Israel; fast messengers were sent to adjacent communities. All

Teveth (29 days)

Shevat (30 days)

Adar (29 days)
(in leap year 30)

Sivan   (30 days)

Nisan   (30 days)

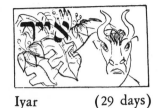

Iyar   (29 days)

reckoning of time, whether for personal or business reasons, or to assure observance of the correct festival days, was based on these reports. Now, this method of computation created discrepancies between the solar, or sun's year, and the lunar, or moon's year. So just as we today have leap years in order to make up for the fraction of a day lost by the ordinary year in reckoning the earth's movement around the sun, the Jews established leap years in which they included not one extra day, but an additional month after Adar. This, called *Adar Sheni* (Second Adar), appears in seven out of every cycle of nineteen years. Though our holiday dates still vary, they occur at approximately the same period of the generally observed calendar. And *Rosh Hodesh*, which sometimes also includes the last day of the previous month, is celebrated as a time of rejoicing and as a renewal (this is what *Hodesh* really means) of all that is good in Jewish life and teaching. Our prayers thank God for His benevolence in "daily renewing the work of creation."

Tamuz   (29 days)

In the Book of Genesis, for each day of creation the phrase is used "and it was evening, and it was morning." For this reason Jews have always reckoned the day from sundown to sundown. We begin the Sabbath and the festivals with the previous evening sunset, and end them when the stars appear for the concluding evening service. This fact is first learned by the Jewish child in observance of the Sabbath — holiest day of the Jewish calendar.

Av   (30 days)

Elul   (29 days)

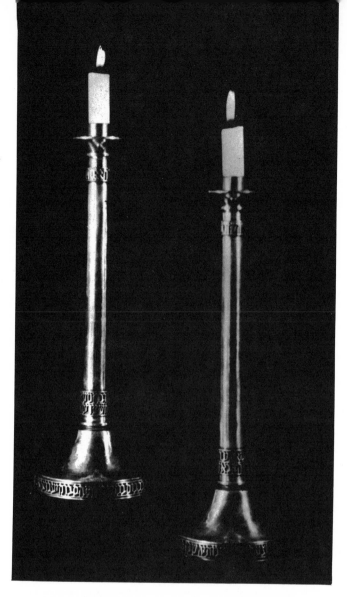

CANDLESTICKS, designed at Arts & Crafts School, Bezalel Institute, Jerusalem, Silver with cutout Hebrew lettering, Courtesy, American Funds for Israel Institutions

REMEMBER THE SABBATH

Remember the sabbath day, to keep it holy. Six days shalt thou labour, and do all thy work; but the seventh day is a sabbath unto the Lord thy God, in it thou shalt not do any manner of work, thou, nor thy son, nor thy daughter, nor thy man-servant, nor thy maid-servant, nor thy cattle, nor thy stranger that is within thy gates; for in six days the Lord made heaven and earth, the sea, and all that in them is, and rested on the seventh day; wherefore the Lord blessed the sabbath day, and hallowed it.

Exod. 20: 8-11

And the heaven and the earth were finished, and all the host of them. And on the seventh day God finished His work which He had made; and He rested on the seventh day from all His work which He had made. And God blessed the seventh day, and hallowed it; because that in it He rested from all His work which God in creating had made.

Gen. 2: 1-3

Wherefore the children of Israel shall keep the sabbath, to observe the sabbath throughout their generations, for a perpetual covenant. It is a sign between Me and the children of Israel for ever; for in six days the Lord made heaven and earth, and on the seventh day He ceased from work and rested.

Exod. 31: 16-17

62

"THE FATHER RETURNS FROM THE SYNAGOGUE ON FRIDAY EVENING" Woodcut by Ilya Schor
Midrashic lore relates that two angels, one good, the other bad, accompany the father on his return from
the synagogue. The sanctity and delight of the Sabbath in the home overwhelms the bad angel who,
against his will, responds "Amen" to the father's chanting of "Shalom Aleichem."

The only festive observance ordered by the Ten Commandments is that of the
Sabbath (*Shabbat*). The greatness of the day is stressed in all the sacred writings
of Israel. In the Talmud we read: "The Holy One, blessed is He, spake unto Moses,
'I have a precious gift in my treasure house, and Sabbath is its name. I wish to
present it to Israel. Go and bring them the good tidings."

This day of rest and holiness was not only a gift to Israel. It was the first time in
human history that every seventh day was set aside for sanctity and repose. Some
nations of antiquity had no rest days whatever. Other religions derived from Judaism, though observing a different day of the week, adapted the Sabbath idea from the
Jews. When the leaders of the French Revolution tried to overturn previous custom and employ the decimal system even in matters of work cessation, making
every tenth day the period of rest, they found it necessary to return to the custom
of the seventh day rest. They discovered that one out of seven was the minimum required by any worker to do his best and preserve his health.

There are two versions of the Ten Commandments in the Bible. In the first
(Exodus 20) we are enjoined: "Remember the Sabbath day, to keep it holy . . . .
for in six days the Lord made heaven and earth, the sea, and all that in them is, and
rested on the seventh day; wherefore the Lord blessed the Sabbath day, and

63

KIDDUSH CUP (from Frankfort Synagogue) Frankfort—on—the— Main, Germany, 1600. Gold. Inscriptions from Exodus and Deuteronomy. Recovered with other Nazi loot by The Jewish Cultural Reconstruction, Inc., and in 1951 given to The Jewish Museum, New York City

KIDDUSH CUP FOR THE SYNAGOGUE,
by William B. Meyers, Newark, N. J.
Silver with bead edges and grape cluster
ornamentations; bowl lined with gold.
Courtesy, Union of American Hebrew Congregations, New York City

WINE CARAFE, Moravia, 1740, Bezalel Museum, Jerusalem.
Courtesy, American Fund for Israel Institutions

KIDDUSH CUP, Augsberg, Germany, 18th century
Silver, gilded and chased. Inscription:
"Remember the Sabbath Day to keep it holy.
Remember it with a blessing over wine."
Courtesy, The Jewish Museum, New York City

PLATE FOR WINE CUP by Ilya Schor. Silver, engraved and appliqued, with inscription giving the blessing
over the wine.
Courtesy, Dr. and Mrs. A. Kanof, Brooklyn, New York

hallowed it." In the variant (Deuteronomy 5) we read: "Observe the Sabbath day, to keep it holy . . . . And thou shalt remember that thou wast a servant in the land of Egypt, and the Lord thy God brought thee out of thence . . . . therefore the Lord thy God commanded thee to keep the sabbath day."

From these declarations we understand that men are to rest from all their weekday activities — but not solely because physical rest is a human necessity. Thought must be directed to God and His creation. By remembering the cruel enslavement of man by man, each person attains a social attitude toward all others. He recognizes the importance of social justice, of freedom and understanding. For one God is the creator of all things and of all men. When men find respite from the toil and turmoil of the week, they should contemplate things of the spirit — study, prayer, introspection.

To the Jew the benefits of the Sabbath must be extended to all persons with whom he has any relationship whatever. "In it thou shalt not do any manner of work, thou, nor thy son, nor thy daughter, nor thy man-servant, nor thy maid-servant, nor thy cattle, nor thy stranger that is within thy gates" — so that they "may rest as well as thou." Here is the first expression of Jewish universalism, disclosing the biblical inclusion of all God's children in the teachings and traditions and practices of Judaic social justice.

. . . . "And call the Sabbath a delight."   Is. 58:13.

"SABBATH REST" by Moritz Oppenheim, "

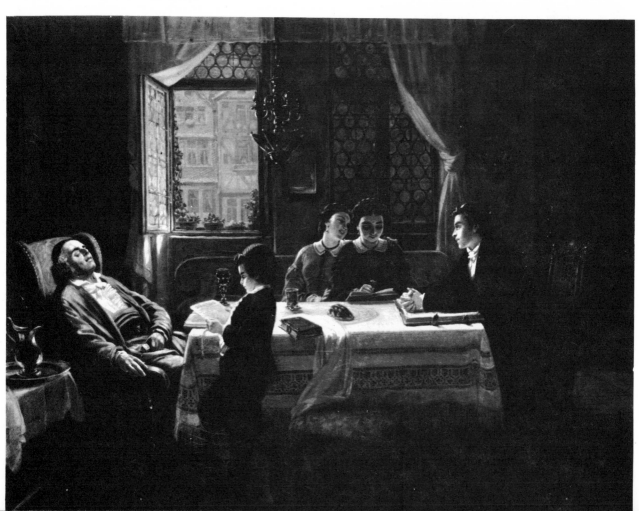

PITCHER, Oriental, late 18th century. Silver, hammered, and engraved.
Courtesy, collection of Louis S. Werner, New York City.

During most of the centuries of Jewish life, the people of Israel observed the
Sabbath to the fullest. The best foods, the best clothes, the best of everything, were
reserved for the holy day. The laws designed to prevent infractions of full rest were
scrupulously observed. No power could weaken the Jewish resolve to sanctify
the day. The Talmud tells of a Roman emperor who boasted that he was as powerful as God. A Jewish sage suggested that he order all fires to be extinguished on a

certain day. Yet from the palace one could see wisps of smoke from many chimneys. Said the sage, "Your majesty, you have immediate power of life and death over your subjects. Yet they disobey you. But God ordered the Jews not to kindle flame on the Sabbath; and when you look at the Jewish homes on that day you will find none in which this command was broken."

So strong has been the influence of the Sabbath in shaping the life and destiny of the Jewish people.

The idea of the seventh day was extended far beyond the limits of the week. The Torah commanded that all slaves be freed and compensated after seven years, to assume the roles of free men. On the jubilee year, not only were slaves to be liberated, but all real property that had been sold was to revert to the former owners — thus equalizing the general economy.

Everything done during the week is by the Jews considered anticipatory and preparatory for the Sabbath. The other days have no names in the Hebrew calendar, only numbers (first day, second day) — they advance progressively to the final sanctity of *Shabbat*. Great preparations are made in the home; since there can be no cooking on the Sabbath itself, all food for the traditional three meals is ready before nightfall on Friday, when the candles are blessed by the mother of the household. Thus the house is already sanctified while the male worshipers are at the synagogue.

At the synagogue the day is greeted lovingly, bearing the poetic figures of "Queen" and "Bride." Before the common evening prayers are recited, there is a service of *Kabbalat Shabbat,* welcoming the Sabbath. This contains an acrostic hymn for Friday eve by Rabbi Solomon Halevi Alkabetz (16c.), with the refrain, "Come, my friend, to meet the bride; let us welcome the presence of the Sabbath."

Kiddush, or the Sabbath and festival sanctification over wine, is first recited at the synagogue. For in ancient and even comparatively recent days travelers and poor folk ate and slept in the vestry rooms, making the house of worship their temporary home.

The returning worshipers find their home and table spiritually and physically glorified. The candles gleam; the table is set with a handsome cloth; all is prepared for the symbolic Queen. The father chants a hymn to the heavenly beings: "Come in peace, angels of peace, messengers from on high." He blesses his children, and chants the thirty-first chapter of Proverbs, exalting the woman of worth and valor. The evening is a time for rest at home, or some study of sacred lore.

The custom of studying the biblical portion of the week is carried out in the morning before the family leaves for the synagogue. At the synagogue there is a morning service *(Shaharit),* followed by the formal reading of the weekly portion of the Torah and related chapters from the Prophets. Thus, during the year, the entire Pentateuch (Five Books of Moses), is certain to be read — an achievement

SPICE CONTAINER by William B. Meyers, Newark, N. J.
Silver, bead edge and grape cluster ornamentation.
Courtesy, Union of Hebrew Congregations, New York City

SPICE CONTAINER (tower form), 17th century,
Silver filigree, In Bezalel Museum, Jerusalem.
Courtesy, American Fund for Israel Institutions

celebrated on the festival of *Simhat Torah*. Then comes *Musaf* (an additional service) which generally is concluded with a hymn glorifying the Creator of the universe.

The noon meal is also preceded by a *kiddush*. A third meal (*Shalosh Seudot*) is prescribed for the period between the afternoon (*Minhah*) and evening (*Maariv*) services. When the evening prayer is concluded after nightfall, the *Havdalah* ("division") blessing is chanted over wine to mark the separation of the Sabbath from the weekdays, and the beginning of a new and, we hope, of a "good week." In addition to the blessing over wine, there are benedictions over spice (in a special container of wood or metal), since spice was used at the end of a meal in olden days; and over candle or other light, since now it is permitted once more to kindle lights. At home *Havdalah* is recited by the father for the benefit of all the family.

HAVDALAH SET, by H. David Gumbel, contemporary Israeli silversmith. Silver, with cutout Hebrew lettering, In Bezalel Museum, Jerusalem.
Courtesy, American Fund for Israel Institutions

Sabbath observances were never considered a hardship or limitation by religious Jews. They are the means for proper exaltation of the holiest day and of the "additional soul" each observant Jew is presumed to have gained with the Sabbath advent.

On the Sabbath *Zemirot,* songs expressing the spirit of the day, and hymns are chanted at the table. A free rendition of one of these is — *Yom Zeh Mechubad* ("*Honored is this day*"):

> This day above all other days is blessed,
> For on it did the Lord God choose to rest.
> Six days in toil and work are spent;
> The seventh day for God is meant.
> So cease from toil; crown His intent
> Who made the world at His behest.
> The heavens e'er proclaim God's praise;
> The earth His love and grace displays.
> He made all creatures, rules their ways;
> Perfection, all His works attest.

70

There are specially named Sabbaths in the Jewish year, on which variant readings from the Torah and the Prophets are substituted.

The first Sabbath after *Simhat Torah* is called *Shabbat Bereshit,* which is the first Hebrew word in the Bible — for then the reading of the Torah begins anew.

Shabbat Shirah ("song") is that on which the portion *Beshallah,* containing the Song of Moses, is read. This Sabbath generally comes in *Shevat* (early February).

On *Shabbat Shekalim,* which occurs in Adar (late February), there is an additional reading concerning the prescribed giving of the shekel.

The Sabbath before Purim is *Shabbat Zakhor,* after the Torah reading — which begins *Zakhor* ("Remember") what Amalek did.

On the Sabbath after Purim the laws of the red heifer *("parah")* are read, hence it is called *Shabbat Parah.*

Shabbat ha-Hodesh ("the month") is celebrated just before the first of *Nisan,* month of Passover.

Before Tish ah B'av comes *Shabbat Hazon,* so named after the first word in Isaiah (prophetic reading of that Sabbath.) After Tish ah B'Av comes *Shabbat Nahamu,* for the first word in Isaiah 40 (the Sabbath's *haftarah*) — "Comfort ye, my people."

Shabbat Teshuvah is the one between *Rosh Hashanah* and *Yom Kippur.* Any Sabbath coinciding with the New Moon is called *Shabbat Rosh Hodesh.*
(Sukkot — The Feast of Tabernacles, the Season of Our Gladness)

MOSAIC, by A. Raymond Katz. On the facade of the Ahi Ezer Synagogue, Brooklyn, New York

On Sabbath afternoons, between Passover and Rosh Hashanah, it is customary to read a chapter from Pirke Aboth, generally translated as Ethics (or Sayings) of the Fathers. Aboth is one of the sixty-three tractates of the Mishnah. The excerpts that follow are ethical pronunciamentos of the sages who flourished between 300 B. C. E. and 200 C. E.

Upon three things the world is based: upon the Torah, upon the Temple service, and upon the practice of charity.   1:2

Provide thyself a teacher, and get thee a companion, and judge all men in the scale of merit.

1:6

He used to say, If I am not for myself, who will be for me?

And being for my own self, what am I? And if not now, when?   1:14

Fix a period for thy study of the Torah; say little and do much; and receive all men with a cheerful countenance.   1:15

By three things is the world preserved: by truth, by judgment, and by peace.   1:18

Hillel said: Separate not thyself from the congregation; trust not in thyself until the day of thy death; judge not thy neighbor until thou art come into his place; and say not anything which cannot be understood at once, in the hope that it will be understood in the end; neither say, When I have leisure, I will study; perchance thou wilt have no leisure. 2:5

Where there is no Torah, there are no manners; where there are no manners, there is no Torah; where there is no wisdom, there is no fear of God; where there is no fear of God, there is no wisdom; where there is no knowledge, there is no understanding; where there is no understanding there is no knowledge; where there is no meal there is no Torah; where there is no Torah there is no meal. 3:21

Who is wise? He who learns from all men, as it is said, From all my teachers I have gotten understanding (Psalms 119:99). Who is mighty? He who subdues his passions, as it is said, He that is slow to anger is better than the mighty, and he that ruleth over his spirit than he that taketh a city (Prov. 16:32). Who is rich? He who rejoices in his portion, as it is said, When thou eatest the labor of thine hands, happy art thou, and it shall be well with thee (Psalms 128:2); happy art thou in this world, and it shall be well with thee in the world to come. Who is honored? He who honors others, as it is said, For them that honor me I will honor, and they that despise me shall be held in contempt (I Sam. 2:30). 4:1

There are seven marks of an uncultured, and seven of a wise man. The wise man does not speak before him who is greater than he in wisdom; and does not break in upon the speech of his fellow; he is not hasty to answer; he questions according to the subject matter, and answers to the point; he speaks upon the first thing first and the last last; regarding that which he has not understood he says, I do not understand it, and he acknowledges the truth. The reverse of all this is to be found in an uncultured man. 5:10

The Torah is greater than the priesthood and than royalty, seeing that royalty demands thirty qualifications, the priesthood twenty-four, while the Torah is acquired by forty-eight. And these are they: By audible study; by distinct pronunciation; by understanding and discernment of the heart; by awe, reverence, meekness, cheerfulness; by ministering to the sages, by attaching oneself to colleagues, by discussion with disciples; by sedateness; by knowledge of Scripture and the Mishnah; by moderation in business, in intercourse with the world, in pleasure, in sleep, in conversation, in laughter; by long-suffering; by a good heart; by faith in the wise; by resignation under chastisement; by recognizing one's place, rejoicing in one's portion, putting a fence to one's words, claiming no merit for oneself; by being beloved, loving the All-present, loving mankind, loving just courses, rectitude, and reproof; by keeping oneself far from honor; not boasting of one's learning, nor delighting in giving decisions; by bearing the yoke with one's fellow, judging him favorably, and leading him to truth and peace; by being composed in one's study; by asking and answering, hearing and adding thereto (by one's own reflection); by learning with the object of teaching, and by learning with the object of practising; by making one's master wiser, fixing attention upon his discourse, and reporting a thing in the name of him who said it. So thou hast learnt, Whosoever reports a thing in the name of him that said it brings deliverance into the world; as it is said, And Esther told the king in the name of Mordecai (Esther 2:22). 6:6

FOR I GIVE YOU GOOD DOC-
TRINE; FORSAKE YE NOT MY
TEACHING. IT IS A TREE OF
LIFE TO THEM THAT GRASP
IT, AND OF THEM THAT UP-
HOLD IT EVERY ONE IS REN-
DERED HAPPY. ITS WAYS
ARE WAYS OF PLEASANTNESS,
AND ALL ITS PATHS ARE
PEACE. TURN THOU US UNTO
THEE, O LORD, AND WE
SHALL RETURN; RENEW OUR
DAYS AS OF OLD.

from Sabbath Morning Service

TORAH WITH MANTLE, HEADPIECES, BREASTPLATE, AND POINTER, by William B. Meyers, Newark, New Jersey.

ROSH HASHANAH

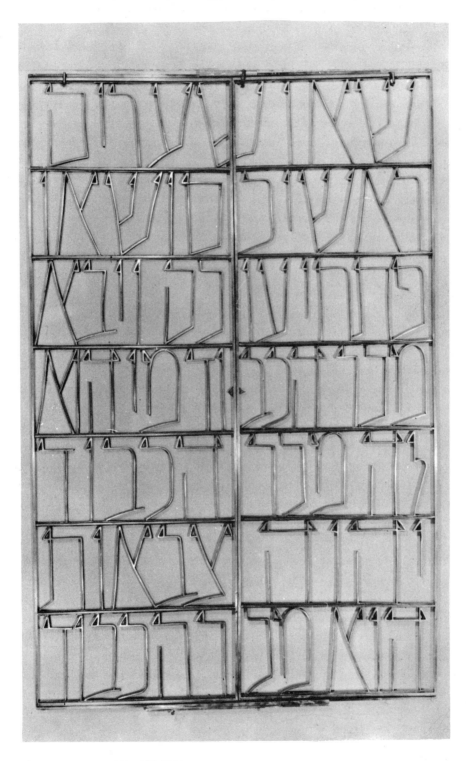

DOORS FOR THE HOLY TORAH ARK
Brass, formed of modern Hebrew lettering, the text taken from Chapter 24 of Psalms, " . . . lift up your heads, O ye gates . . . that the King of Glory may come in . . . " In the Bezalel Museum, Jerusalem
Courtesy, American Fund for Israel Institutions

The first day of the Hebrew month *Tishri*, which comes in the fall, is the Jewish New Year. The name *Rosh Hashanah* ("head of the year") is not given in the Bible, which calls it instead *Yom Teruah* or *Zichron Teruah* — "day of sounding the shofar" or "memorial of the sounding of the shofar" (ram's horn). Other names, found in our holiday prayerbook, are *Yom ha-Zikkaron* and *Yom ha-Din* — "day of memorial" and "day of judgment." The Jewish New Year has a variety of meanings and observances, and each of its names refers to a special significance.

After the Exodus from Egypt, the month of *Nissan,* on which Passover occurs, was generally accepted as Israel's first month. But it appears that in the earliest days *Tishri* was first. The difficulties in establishing the calendar, already mentioned, extended the observance from one to two days; and even in Israel, which observes but one instead of two days on other holidays, the two days of *Rosh Hashanah* are retained. The Hebrew word for repentance is *teshuvah* — "turning" — denoting the genuine change of heart which impels the sinner to turn from evil, and return to God. *Rosh Hashanah* begins a ten day period of repentance, during which "the remembrance of every creature, man's deeds and destiny, his works and ways, his thoughts and designs" are forcefully brought to mind. And since recalling the missteps of the year past creates problems of conscience, *Rosh Hashanah* adds to the thought of memory the idea of judgment. Each man must judge his own actions, and take steps to eradicate personal sins and errors as well as injuries done one's fellowman. God will forgive or punish transgressions against Him as He sees fit; our primary concern is to conduct ourselves in a Godly manner toward our brethren on earth, who are all God's children.

The outstanding and best remembered custom of *Rosh Hashanah* is the sounding of the *shofar,* whose weird notes from the oldest of wind instruments are designed to awaken all worshipers to the need for prayer and repentance. The *shofar* was sounded at Mount Sinai; it was employed to herald the year of jubilee. It proclaimed many other historical and ritual observances, and it was used as a warning of immediate danger.

There are one hundred blasts prescribed in the *mahzor* (holiday prayerbook). They are heard in the latter portions of the morning services, probably because children and laggards will all be present during the final hours. The notes announced before each sounding are *tekiah*, the single blast; *shevarim*, a three-part broken blast; and *teruah,* a rapid succession of short notes. All the notes are calculated to rouse men's consciences, bring searching of hearts, and assure meditation on improving one's way in life. The ram's horn is used because, when Abraham was about to express his supreme faith by offering up his son Isaac, it was a ram caught in the bushes which became the substitute sacrifice.

On the day when all mankind is to pass in judgment before God, it also

ROSH HASHANAH PLATE, Holland, circa 1700
Faience, blue and white
On the eve of the New Year used for serving an apple dipped in honey
Courtesy, The Jewish Museum, New York City

expresses every important teaching and future hope of the people of Israel. Saadia Gaon (892-942) saw in the *shofar* blast intimations of the following episodes to God, the revelation on Mount Sinai, and duties: the Creation, the sinner's return the exhortations of the prophets, the destruction of the Temple, Abraham's binding of Isaac for the sacrifice, alertness to peril, conscience and judgment, Israel's redemption, and life eternal.

77

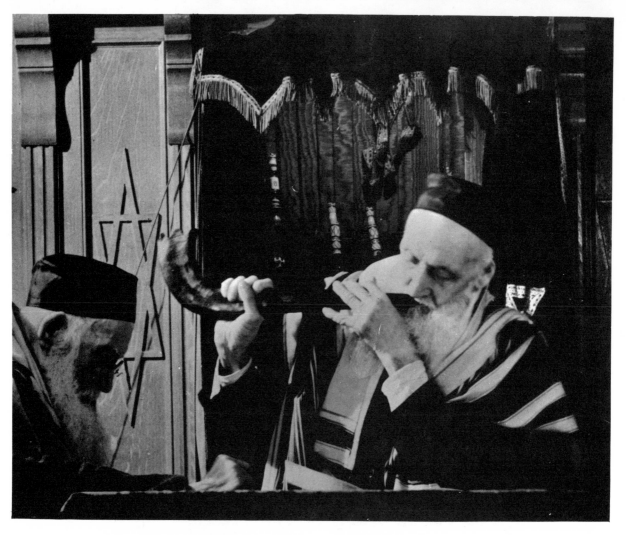

SOUNDING THE SHOFAR
" . . . Shall the shofar be blown in the city, and the people not tremble?" *Amos 3:6*

Rosh Hashanah prayers recognize the truth that man is frail, and always in need of repentance for past misdeeds. They dramatize the Jewish precept that man must take continuous stock of himself and his acts, and not only on days set aside for that purpose. We are exhorted by our liturgy to find the blame for our hardships in ourselves — but we add a note of hopefulness to our plaints. For ultimately "the upright will be glad . . . . and Thou shalt remove the dominion of evil from the earth."

At meals on *Rosh Hashanah* bread is dipped in honey as a symbol of a sweeter and better year to come. A new fruit is tasted, so as further to justify our thanks to God for giving us life to this time and renewing our spiritual power. Sin in itself is overpowering; and one widely practised custom is that of *tashlikh* — the "casting away" of sin, through symbolic rites by a running stream.

Many special hymns and poems are recited on *Rosh Hashanah*, most of them composed during medieval times. The most important of these, read also on *Yom*

78

Kippur, is *Unetaneh Tokef,* composed by Rabbi Amnon of Mayence. According to the story related in the centuries following, Amnon was pressed by the local bishop to accept conversion. Once, instead of an immediate refusal to follow the bishop's behest, he begged for three days to consider. For this hesitation he felt so guilty that when summoned to the bishop's presence he asked that his tongue be cut off. Instead, the priest had the rabbi's hands and feet amputated. As the story continues, Rabbi Amnon requested to be brought into the synagogue. When the *kedushah,* or sanctification service read by cantor and congregation, was about to begin, he asked permission to offer a prayer he had written. Immediately afterward, he passed away.

Rabbi Amnon's prayer, which gives expression to the mystic idea inherent in the *Rosh Hashanah* services, may well close any description of the Jewish New Year:

"We will celebrate the mighty holiness of this day, a day of awe and terror, a day on which Thy Kingdom is exalted and Thy throne established in mercy, on which Thou sittest in truth. Verily Thou art the judge and arbiter Who knowest all, and bearest witness, and writest and sealest and recordest, and reckonest. Thou rememberest all forgotten things. Thou openest the Book of Records from which the accounting is read, attested by the seal of every man. A great trumpet is sounded, and a still, small voice is heard. Even the angels are dismayed, for fear and trembling have seized them, as they proclaim: This is the day of judgment whereon the heavenly host is arraigned in judgment, for even they are not pure in Thine eyes; and all who enter the world Thou dost cause to pass before Thee as a flock of sheep. Yea, even as a shepherd mustereth his flock and passeth his lambs beneath the crook, so dost Thou cause to pass, and number and count and visit, every living soul, appointing to each of Thy creatures the measure of their days and writing down their destiny.

"On the New Year it is written, and on the Day of Atonement it is sealed, how many are to pass away and how many to be born; who shall live and who shall die; to whom shall be granted the full time allotted to man and who shall be taken before his course is run; who is to perish by fire and who by water; who by the sword and who by wild beasts; who by hunger and who by thirst; who by earthquake and who by plague; who by strangling and who by stoning; who shall be at rest and who displaced; who shall be tranquil and who disturbed; who shall be at ease and who chastened; who shall become poor and who enriched; who shall be abased and who uplifted.

"BUT PENITENCE, PRAYER, AND CHARITY
AVERT THE EVIL DECREE!"

DAYS OF PENITENCE

There are ten days of *teshuvah* — "turning" or "penitence" — beginning with *Rosh Hashanah* and ending with *Yom Kippur*. During all this time the spiritual stocktaking enjoined upon every Jew must continue. For the rabbis understood that taking account of our conduct and altering our future for the better are not easy tasks. Men are creatures of habit, even when they are aware that the habits are bad and destructive. To the teachers of Israel there could never be too much *teshuvah*.

The *asseret yeme teshuvah,* this important ten-day period, is to be approached with three aims — abandonment of the wrongful path, honest remorse, and an active effort to achieve atonement by good deeds. The Talmud tells of three books being opened in heaven. One is for the completely righteous, who are at once inscribed in the book of life; another is for the wholly wicked, who are in the book of the condemned. The third is for the great mass of indeterminate humans whose doom is suspended during these ten days; and according to his deserts each is then inscribed in the book of life or is condemned.

The Sabbath falling within the ten days is called *Shabbat Shuvah*, since the prophetic reading for the day begins with the words. *Shuvah Yisrael* — "Return, O Israel, unto the Lord thy God." It has been the custom for rabbis to deliver lengthy discourses on human life and morals on this Sabbath.

There are insertions in the congregational prayers throughout the period, which briefly plead for the worshiper's inclusion in the book of life. A series of supplications each beginning *Avinu Malkenu* — "Our Father, our King" — is recited twice a day.

And it shall come to pass in the end of days,

That the mountain of the Lord's house shall be established

as the top of the mountains,

And shall be exalted above the hills;

And all nations shall flow unto it.

And many peoples shall go and say:

'Come ye, and let us go up to the mountain of the Lord,

To the house of the God of Jacob;

And He will teach us of His ways,

And we will walk in His paths.'

For out of Zion shall go forth the law,

And the word of the Lord from Jerusalem.

And He shall judge between the nations,

And shall decide for many peoples;

And they shall beat their swords into plowshares

And their spears into pruning-hooks;

Nation shall not lift up sword against nation,

Neither shall they learn war any more.

Isaiah 2:2-4

"AND THEY SHALL BEAT THEIR SWORDS INTO PLOWSHARES . . . " *(Is. 2:4)*
Sculpture by Moissaye Marans, Brooklyn, New York
Reproduced through courtesy of the Architectural League, New York City

YOM KIPPUR

Yom Kippur, which climaxes the ten days of penitence, is observed by fasting and prayer for over twenty-four hours. The Bible orders all Jews to "afflict" themselves during this day of repentance, and affliction has been expounded as abstaining from food, the least harmful of possible self-injuries. After eating a festive meal in broad daylight, the worshiper arrives at the synagogue while it is still light. He leaves the house of worship the next evening after dark, following recital of the regular evening prayer. Except where illness prevents, or the person is too young or too old, no food or drink is taken through the entire period.

Yet at no time is there anything fearsome about the Day of Atonement. The worshiper feels that he is carrying out one of the finest behests of his religion. The same restraint of appetite applying to food, can be translated to conduct conducive to sin. The penitent learns that will power can overcome temptation, and this lesson is applied to his daily conduct.

Throughout the service it is stressed that *Yom Kippur* atones only for sins against God, "but for transgressions against a fellowman the Day of Atonement does not atone, unless and until he has conciliated his fellowman, and redressed the wrong he has done him."

Quite naturally the outstanding day of the Jewish year must have many unique customs. Men wear *kittels* (white gowns) representing the ideal of purity. Shoes are removed, to emulate the custom of the ancient priests when they trod holy ground. There are special blessings for one's children and other distinctive acts.

Nothing in the day's customs and liturgy even remotely approaches the uniqueness of the extraordinary special service for the first moments of the fastday, known as *Kol Nidre* ("All vows"). This is chanted three times, beginning while there still is light. It is sung to one of the most distinctive melodies known to man, plaintive, beautiful, appealing. This prayer was composed in the early centuries of the present era. Long after, when Spain persecuted the Jews under Ferdinand

and Isabella, on *Yom Kippur*, these forced converts (known as Marranos,) would assemble in secret. The elders would then declare that the false oaths imposed upon the congregation were null and void, like any vow made under compulsion. The music was composed to fit the words. Later the custom spread to other lands.

In certain communities of the ninth and tenth centuries, particularly in Arabia, there is no record of the *Kol Nidre* being sung on *Yom Kippur*. But in Spain, where the words originated, the prayer was recited all through the so-called Golden Age under the Moslems. It became significant once more when new persecutions arose in that country. And under the Christian persecutions of Ferdinand and Isabella there was more reason than ever to proclaim the abrogation of forced vows at secret *Yom Kippur* services.

"BETH HAMIDRASH" oil by Isidor Kaufman
Courtesy, Oscar Gruss, New York City

There are two sentences that precede the cantor's rendition of *Kol Nidre*. One is the phrase from Psalms—"Light is sown for the righteous, and gladness for the upright in heart." This is the principle behind all prayers for repentance, which bring light and gladness to all devout men. The other phrase was devised to silence such members of the congregation as might protest the admission into the synagogue of Marranos who had chosen to masquerade as Christians in Spain. Many of these Jews seeking reconversion fled to Amsterdam, Hamburg, and other more northern communities, were the elders devised a formula to silence the objectors: "With the consent of God, and with consent of the congregation, by authority of the court on high, and by authority of the court on earth, we give leave to pray with them that have transgressed."

It must not be forgotten that the oaths from which men could thus be absolved did not cover transgressions against fellowmen, but only those against God and His Law. But many Jew-haters attempted to prove that *Kol Nidre* was a blanket permission for all Jews to violate any promises made to their fellows. It was sometimes necessary to recite an introduction to the prayer clarifying its intent.

There are two "confessionals" in the *Yom Kippur* prayers—*Ashamnu* and *Al Het*—recited several times during the services. Since every possible sin is confessed to God, even by those who have committed no sin whatever, and since the plural is used throughout, the confession is completely impersonal. It covers all the sins of all the congregation, yet no one can ascertain the particular crimes committed by any individual.

Numerous impressive hymns—*piyyutim*—appear in the service of the cantor and congregation. In the additional morning service (*Mussaf*) the *Avodah* (service of the high priest in ancient days) is described in poetic form. The reading from the Torah in the morning applies to the *Yom Kippur* sacrifices in the Temple. The prophetic reading immediately following is from Isaiah 57: it stresses penitence, humility, and peace. There is an added Torah reading during the afternoon service, which consists of the laws of forbidden marriage; on this day the importance of sex morality is strongly proclaimed. The *haftarah*, or prophetic reading, consists mainly of the entire Book of Jonah—for the story of the prophet who fled from God's bidding and then repented illustrates the power and worth of sincere atonement for sin.

Just before the sun begins to set, the special and final *Yom Kippur* service called *Neilah*—"closing"— is chanted. Before the "gates of heaven" are closed, the worshippers pray that they may be "sealed" in the book of life. The day is ended with a final blast of the *shofar*, acceptance of the unity of God, and a hope for restoration of the Holy City of Jerusalem.

"THE SUKKAH" by Moritz Oppenheim, Germany (1800-1882)
"Thou shalt keep the Feast of Tabernacles . . ."
Courtesy, Oscar Gruss, New York City

Two weeks after *Rosh Hashanah,* five days after *Yom Kippur,* begin the nine days known as *Sukkot.* This word means tabernacles or booths — for the ancestors of Israel wandered for long years in the desert, living in booths or temporary huts, before reaching the Promised Land and achieving their independent nationhood. In Leviticus 23:34 we read "on the fifteenth day of this seventh month is the feast of tabernacles for seven days unto the Lord"; and "Ye shall dwell in booths seven days . . . . that your generations may know that I made the children of Israel to dwell in booths, when I brought them out of the land of Egypt" (Lev. 23:42, 43).

Insomuch as the *sukkah* built in the centuries thereafter by observant Jews was to be a symbol of God's goodness in times of stress, and of the faith that sustained the wanderers, each hut has to conform with certain stringent rules. It must be not higher than twenty cubits (about thirty feet), nor lower than ten handbreadths — teaching that man should become neither overly haughty nor excessively humble and subservient. There must be more shade than sun, as a means for intensifying the lessons of steadfastness and humility, as distinct from the misleading glare of the world at large. The latticed roof may be covered only with broken leaves and branches, through which the stars may be seen. These are reminders of Israel's eternal Guardian. And within are hung fruits and vegetables, indicating the bounties of the Lord.

Since this is the season of the harvest, the festival is also known as *Hag he-Asif,* Feast of the Ingathering. The Lord is thanked at religious services not only through prayer, but through the use of four species ordained by the Bible itself. We bring together the *etrog,* or citron; the *lulav,* palm branch; *hadassim,* myrtle; and *aravot,* willow, both as agricultural symbols and as representing the four kinds of men making up the nation, or any nation. According to the Midrash, the *etrog* has both taste and a good odor, signifying those who are both learned and religiously observant. The *lulav* has fruit that can be eaten, but no fragrance — like the learned ones who do not carry out the precepts of their faith. The myrtle, which has a good odor but no taste, is like the men of good and pious deeds who possess no scholarship. And the willow, lacking both food value and fragrance, refers to such as have neither learning nor good deeds.

Every day but the Sabbath the four species are part of the religious service. At prescribed times they are pointed in all directions, thus proclaiming the dominion of God in all places on earth. Carrying these four species, worshipers make circuits *(hakafot)* within the synagogue — chanting prayers of praise, thanksgiving, and trust in the Lord.

Now in olden days it was declared that on this festival judgment was passed on the coming of rain. Hence in the Land of Israel there was a brilliant colorful ceremony of water drawing — *simhat bet ha-shoevah* — fully described in the Talmud, and now being reenacted in the new State. And every seven years, com-

SUKKAH WITH WALL PAINTING, Bavaria, circa 1820.
After World War II the original wooden boards were sent to Jerusalem from Bavaria and reconstructed in the Jewish National Museum, Bezalel. Note photograph of interior of *sukkah* for close-up of wall paintings of German and Jerusalem landscapes.

"BLESSING ON TAKING THE LULAV" pen and ink by H. Felix Kraus, New York

mands the Bible, Israel is to assemble (*hakhel*) on *Sukkot* for instruction. For the first time in centuries such a celebration was conducted in the new Israel during *Sukkot* of 1952.

The seventh day of *Sukkot* is known as *Hoshana Rabba,* because of the large number of chants beginning with the word *hoshana* (save!) that mark the special processions within the synagogue. Willow branches are then beaten, until all leaves are broken off — symbolizing the hope that after the trees and plants lose their leaves God will provide new warmth and moisture for the renewal of nature, man's strength, and man's trust in the Divine.

Then comes *Shemini Atzeret,* the Eighth Day of Solemn Assembly. This is designated by the sages as a distinct festival, not connected with *Sukkot* itself. It is marked by special sacrifices, benedictions, and psalm reading. It is also signalized by special jubilation, although all the days are known as *zeman simhatenu,* the season of our rejoicing. There are dancing and singing, such as Jerusalem witnessed in centuries past. The major feature of the service is the prayer for rain, chanted by the cantor in the same kind of white garment and similar tones employed on *Yom Kippur.* For without rain life could not exist in the land; and the rainy season was

88

"THE FOUR SPECIES" oil painting by Ilya Schor,
Painting is in the Har Zion Temple, Philadelphia, Pennsylvania

ETHROG CONTAINER by Ilya Schor, New York City
Silver, engraved and appliqued
Courtesy, Siegfried Bendheim, New York City

"SIMHAT TORAH" oil painting by Solomon Alexander Hart (1806-1881), England, 1842. Interior of Synagogue of Livorno, Italy.
Courtesy, Oscar Gruss, New York City.

"This Feast of the law all your gladness
  display,
  Today all your homages render.
What profit can lead one so pleasant a
  way,
  What jewels can vie with its splendor?
Then exult on the Law on its festival
  day;
  The Law is our light and defender."

"SIMHAT TORAH" woodcut by Ilya Schor, New York City

always welcomed with prayer and gladness. On this day Jews throughout the world begin to interpolate in the *Shemoneh Esreh* (Eighteen Benediction) prayer the phrase, "Thou causest the wind to blow and the rain to fall."

The ninth day is known as *Simhat Torah* — Rejoicing of the Law — (in Israel it is observed together with *Shemini Atzeret*). The joy is created by the fact that on this day the annual Sabbath reading of the Five Books of Moses is completed, and the new cycle begun. The Torah, which has been called a "traveling fatherland," has been the guide and protection of the people of Israel through all their hardships and wanderings. At the services all the Torah scrolls are taken from the Ark and borne about the synagogue, with song and dance — both in the evening and the morning. Every man has the honor of ascending to the reading of the scrolls, even the young lads, reciting the proper benedictions.

There are two special honors accorded those called to the reading. The person to whom is assigned the final passage of the Torah is the *Hatan Torah* — bridegroom of the Torah. He who begins the reading of the Five Books of Moses anew is known as the *Hatan Bereshit* — bridegroom of Genesis. These honors are customarily given to men of learning and piety, for the close association of the final and initial readings of the Pentateuch are an indication of the eternity of God's revelation and the perpetuity of the people of Israel.

92

TORAH DRESSED WITH MAN-
TLE, CROWN, BREASTPLATE
AND POINTER

Mantle: Brocade and velvet, Ger-
  many, 1765
Crown: Silver, Poland, 18th century
Breastplate: Silver, Galicia, 1870
Pointer: Silver, Galicia, early 19th
  century
Courtesy, The Jewish Museum, New
  York City

HANUKKAH

After the death of Alexander the Great (323 B.C.E.), and the split-up of the Greek Empire, many of the rulers of Palestine attempted to force the Jews to give up their own religion and customs in favor of the Greek and pagan forms. Some Jews yielded to the powers above them, but most of them refused to become pagans under compulsion. Then a certain cruel king, Antiochus of Syria, determined to use all the power of his position and his armies to destroy the Jewish faith, and to kill those Jews who would not obey his commands.

The thought of worshiping idols or images has always repelled Jews. It is stringently forbidden in the Ten Commandments. Yet Antiochus persisted in setting up statues of Zeus, the chief god of Greece, for the Jews to bow down to. A large image was placed in the Temple of Jerusalem itself. Altars were scattered throughout the land, before which sacrifices were to be offered to the Greek gods. The king forbade observance of the Sabbath, the festivals, or the laws concerning food. Many Jews escaped to the hills and caves; others were put to death by the soldiers. Scrolls of the Torah were destroyed, and their owners killed. The Temple was looted and defiled.

Judas Maccabaeus and his eight hundred warriors defeated in the battle of Elasa after a heroic fight against the superior Seleucid force.
Courtesy, The Harry Levine Foundation

HANUKKAH MENORAH, Germany, early 18th century
Silver with enamel medallions on base
Presented to The Jewish Museum, New York City, by Mrs. Felix M. Warburg, in memory of her father,
Jacob H. Schiff, to whom the lamp belonged.

HANUKKAH DREIDEL

The rebellion began in the little town of Modin. Here a courageous old man named Mattathias struck down a Jew who was obeying a military order to bow down to an idol; and his five sons, led by the famed Judas Maccabeus, slew the soldiers and organized a nationwide revolt. Though vastly outarmed and outnumbered, the Jews defeated the Syrians, and in three years they were again able to enter the holy Temple. This was in the year 165 before the common reckoning.

It is related that there was only one tiny cruse of oil in the structure — seemingly enough for but one day in the sacred eternal lamp. It was the only oil sanctified and sealed by the high priest. But, wondrously enough, it burnt for eight full days! So *Hanukkah*, the Feast of Dedication — or the Feast of Lights — is still celebrated for eight days. It begins on the twenty-fifth of *Kislev*, generally about the middle of December.

In order that all may see and understand the miracle of those ancient days, the candelabrum *(Hanukkiyah)* for the holiday is placed where even those outside may look upon it. As soon as stars appear, the candles (or oil wicks) are kindled with appropriate blessings and hymns. A *shamash* (sexton) or server candle is used to light the first candle, to the far right of the *Hanukkah* lamp. Each night an additional candle is set at the left, the last one being first exposed to the flame. On the eighth night all the candles are illuminated. Altogether, including the "sextons," forty-four are lit during the period.

The consecrated candles may not be used to kindle other candles; therefore the *Shamash*, or server candle, is employed for that purpose. One of the hymns sung is *Maoz Tzur*, known in English as "Rock of Ages."

Hanukkah is important for world history as well, for this marks the first successful insurrection against limitation of religious freedom anywhere in the world. In the words recited in the *Siddur* on the days of Hanukkah *(Al ha-Nissim):* "Thou deliveredst the strong into the hands of the weak, the many into the hands of the few, the impure into the hands of the pure, the wicked into the hands of the righteous, and the arrogant into the hands of them that occupied themselves with Thy Law." It remains an example for all the persecuted and downtrodden peoples of the world, that righteousness and justice will triumph so long as men are dedicated to relighting the flame of God in their homes and their temples.

The Jewish triumph not only preserved Judaism, but thereby paved the way for all modern religion emanating from it.

HANUKKAH LAMPS developed into two distinct types — first, the bench type for use in the home only, the back wall providing the artist with space for decorative ornamentation. The larger Hanukkah menorah was a later development, designed for use in the synagogue . . . . "We kindle these lights on account of the miracles and deliverances and wonders which Thou didst work for our fathers . . ."

MENORAH, Hamburg, 17th century
Courtesy, The Jewish Museum, New York City

THE VICTORY OF THE SPIRIT

Hanukkah, the Feast of the Maccabees, celebrates a victory — not a military victory only, but a victory also of the spirit — over things material. Not a victory only over external enemies, the Greeks; but a victory also over more dangerous internal enemies. A victory of the many over the ease-loving, safe-playing, privileged, powerful few, who in their pliancy would have betrayed the best interests of the people, a victory of democracy over aristocracy.

As part of the eternal world-wide struggle for democracy, the struggle of the Maccabees is of eternal worldwide interest. It is a struggle of the Jews of today as well as of those of two thousand years ago. It is a struggle in which all Americans, non-Jews as well as Jews, should be vitally interested because they are vitally affected.

The Maccabees' victory proved that the Jews — then already an old people — possessed the secret of eternal youth: the ability to rejuvenate itself through courage, hope, enthusiasm, devotion, and self-sacrifice of the plain people.

Louis D. Brandeis (1856-1941)

MENORAH-TOPPED LOOKOUT TOWER
RISES TO THE SKIES, ISRAEL
Courtesy, Jewish National Fund, New York

THE DAY OF CARNAGE

From the beginning of the siege of Jerusalem by the Babylonians in 588 B.C.E. through the slaughter of six million Jews by the Nazis during the second World War, stretches a long period of suffering and ruthless extermination. The beginning of this series of holocausts is marked by a fast day on the tenth of Teveth (Asarah be'Teveth). On that day began the siege of Jerusalem by Nebuchadnezzar. It was fitting that this day should also be designated by world Jewry to commemorate the slaughter of the last war. The destruction of the great Eastern and Central European Jewish civilization was the culminating tragedy of the process begun by the Babylonians almost 2,600 years ago.

This catastrophe, marked officially by the fast day of Asarah be'Teveth, has already become the subject of a vast literature. In Hebrew it is referred to as *Hashoah,* the fearful destruction. As the story unfolds — in books, in memoirs, poetry, and fiction — we catch glimpses of the heroic spirit of Israel in the face of almost certain death. Hitler destroyed the bodies of millions of our brethren, but their spirit he could not cremate. In countless acts of resistance, culminating in the heroic Warsaw uprising, doomed Jews showed their kinship with the heroic forefathers who had defied the brutalitarians of their age — Babylonians, Assyrians, Greeks, Romans, Nazis.

May their memory ever recall the greatness of the prophet's vision of a united humanity, for which they gave their lives.

CHIEF RABBI OF ISRAEL, DR. ISAAC HERZOG, PLANTING THE FIRST TREE IN THE FOREST OF THE SIX MILLION MARTYRS, ISRAEL
Courtesy, Jewish National Fund, New York

יער הקדושים

MARTYRS' FOREST

MARTYRS' FOREST, ISRAEL, Poster
Courtesy, Jewish National Fund, New York

THE LAST DANCE

This happened on the last Simhat Torah, in 1942. Only a handful of Jews had remained alive out of the five hundred thousand, formerly in the Polish capital.

Twenty Jews were gathered in the home of Rabbi Menahem Zemba, the last remaining rabbi in Warsaw, to observe Simhat Torah. Among them was Judah Leib Orlean, former director of the Beth Jacob Teachers' Seminary, who had devoted his life to religious education. At the proper time they brought forth the scrolls of the Torah; and, sorrowfully reciting the verses, which in former years had been joyously chanted, they wearily plodded the *hakafot* about the table.

Suddenly a boy of twelve appeared in the room. This was astonishing, for the Germans had already slain or deported, for extermination, all the Jewish cnildren in the ghetto. Who could he be, and where had he come from? No one knew.

Orlean ran to the boy, and embracing him together with his Torah, cried out, "Young Jew with the holy Torah!" He swept him along in an exultant *hassidic* dance. The others joined the dance one by one, until all had formed a circle about the unknown boy, Orlean, and the Torah.

Bereaved fathers who had lost their entire families danced, with tears rolling down their faces, while the great educator reiterated, "Young Jew with the holy Torah! Young Jew with the holy Torah!"

This was the last dance of the last Jews on the last Simhat Torah in Warsaw.

(from Hillel Seidman's Diary)

HEBREW LETTERING

by Ludwig Yehuda

Wolpert, Jerusalem

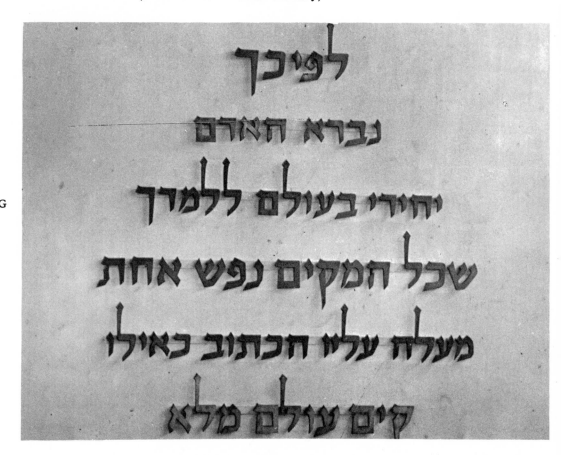

Therefore, but a single man was created in the world, to teach that if any man has caused a single soul to perish from the world, Scripture imputes it to him as though he has caused a whole world to perish; and if man saves alive a single soul from the world, Scripture imputes it to him as though he had saved alive a whole world . . . Maimonides

אֲנִי מַאֲמִין בֶּאֱמוּנָה שְׁלֵמָה בְּבִיאַת הַמָּשִׁיחַ:
וְאַף עַל פִּי שֶׁיִּתְמַהְמֵהַּ, עִם כָּל זֶה אֲנִי מַאֲמִין !

"I BELIEVE WITH PERFECT FAITH IN THE COMING OF THE MES-
SIAH; AND THOUGH HE TARRY, NONE THE LESS DO I BELIEVE."

"THE WAYFARER DREAMS OF THE COMING OF THE MESSIAH"
Painting by Elias Newman, New York City
Collection: Brandeis University, Waltham, Mass.

TU BI'SHEVAT

There is a special New Year for trees in the Jewish calendar. It is called *Hamishah Asar bi'Shevat*, sometimes *Tu bi'Shevat*, because the letters spelling *Tu* have the numerical value of fifteen. The middle of the fifth Jewish month *Shevat*, coming some weeks before the United States has its spring, generally marks the end of Israel's rainy season. The sap becomes active in the trees, and they attain new life and growth.

There is no mention of such a festival in the Bible. Its value was in the fact that it marked the beginning of a new agricultural year in the Holy Land. One tenth — a tithe — of all produce was taken as tax for the Temple and government; since one was not permitted to pay the tithes of one year with produce of another year, it was necessary to set a time for demarcation. This was the beginning of springtime in the Holy Land. With great exultation new trees were planted everywhere. In the Talmud we are told of the custom of planting a cedar sapling for a boy baby, and a cypress for a girl. When they grew up, poles from these trees would be used to hold up their wedding canopies.

In addition to planting, the people celebrate by eating a great variey of fruits on that day. There is song and music and parties for children. Although *Hamishah Asar bi-Shevat* was always considered a semi-festival, in today's Israel it has taken on the character of a national celebration, observed and honored by old and young.

BOYS PLANTING SAPLINGS, ISRAEL
Courtesy, Jewish National Fund, New York

. . "Thou shall not destroy the trees . . . for the tree of the field is man's life."

CHILDREN IN THE CITIES OBSERVE THE HOLIDAY FOR PLANTING (ISRAEL)
Courtesy, Zionist Archives and Library, New York City

"It is forbidden to dwell in a city that has no garden in it." *Talmud Yerushalmi*

" . . . And when ye shall come into the land
and shall have planted all manner of trees . . ."
Lev. 19:23

PURIM

One of the happiest days in the calendar of the Jews is the *Purim* festival, the 14th of *Adar,* whose origin is narrated in the biblical Book of Esther. The deliverance of Persian Jewry from a plot by a highplaced official to exterminate them all, has given the name *Purim* to a great number of local celebrations of days wherein small communities were saved from destruction by some extraordinary event.

But *Purim* itself means "lots," the casting of lots. The emperor of the hundred and twenty-seven provinces of the mighty Persian Empire, Ahasuerus (perhaps Artaxerxes, as we know the name in history), had appointed one Haman as his prime minister. Haman, irked because a certain leading Jew, Mordecai, who worshiped only the God of Israel, would not bow down to him at the king's gate, had the king sign a decree to wipe out all the Jews in the empire. The date for extermination was chosen by lot.

As unusual procession of incidents stayed execution of the decree, brought about the death of Haman and his equally cruel sons, and elevated Mordecai to Haman's high office. For Ahasuerus had sent away his former queen, Vashti, and his chamberlains had spent a year choosing the handsomest lass in Persia as the new queen. This was Esther, who for reasons of security did not at first divulge her origin or Mordecai's until it became necessary to save her people from destruction. Then, on Mordecai's prompting — "Think not . . . that thou shalt escape . . . more than all the Jews . . . and who knoweth whether thou are not come to royal estate

" . . . and that these days of Purim should not fail from among the Jews, nor the memorial of them perish from their seed." *Esther 9:28*

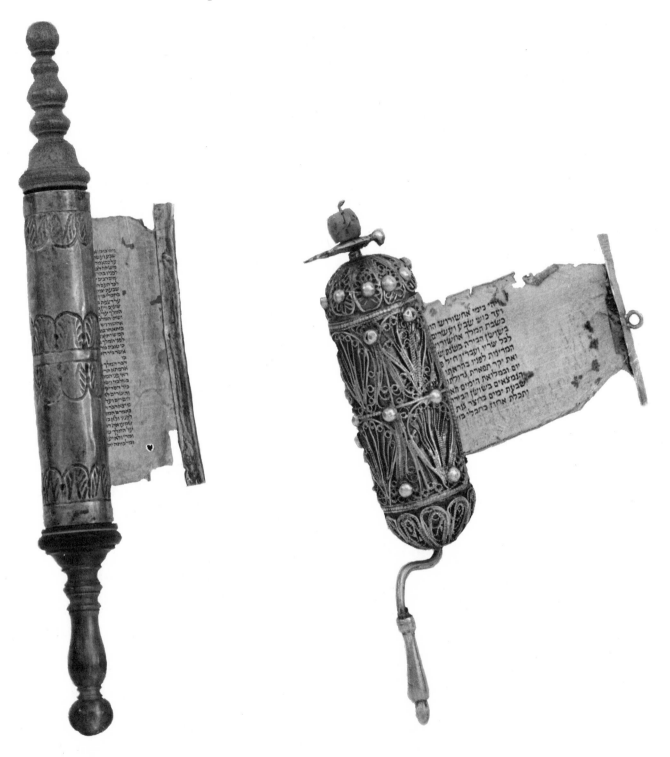

SCROLLS OF ESTHER (MEGILLOTH)
Left: Silver case, Galicia, early 19th century
Right: Silver filigree, Eastern Europe, 18th century

for such a time as this?" — she exposed Haman, the decree was overcome by another permitting the Jews to slay their assailants, and the Jews were accorded new life and honor.

The day before *Purim,* Adar 13, is a fast day, for thereon did Esther and her people fast before the Lord, to avert the evil decree. At evening and morning services the entire scroll of Esther *(Megillah)* is chanted while noisy children grow wild at every mention of Haman's name. They twirl noisemakers, shout, and stamp, and not infrequently go completely out of control. Everyone has a good time, whether youth or adult. Most Jewish schools conduct Purim plays and entertainment. And there is always the Purim *seudah* (feast) to conclude the festival.

The finest observance of the holiday, however, is the custom of sending food to friends and the poor *(mishloah manot).* For thus did our ancestors also celebrate the day — since Jews have always indicated their joyful emotions by giving to charity and bringing light into darkened lives.

The day after *Purim* is called *Shushan Purim.* This is so named because the Jews of Shushan, the capital, were kept busy fighting off their enemies for an additional day.

Many other "Purims" established for later acts of deliverance are observed in Tiberias of Israel, in Egypt, Frankfort, Saragosa, and numerous other places. It is therefore quite correct for a people that has been persecuted in so many times and regions to repeat the dictum of Israel's sages: "While all the other festivals may be annulled, Purim will never disappear."

The hanging of Haman. Copper engraving, Holland, 1725. Gallows with Haman can been seen in the backround.

PESAH

SILVER CANDLESTICK FOR BURNING LEAVEN ON THE EVENING
BEFORE THE PASSOVER SEDER, by Ilya Schor, New York City.
Courtesy, Siegfried Bendheim, New York City
"All manner of leaven that is in my possession, which I have not seen or
removed, shall be considered null and void, and accounted as the dust of the
earth" (recited after the search for leaven).

PASSOVER PLATE, Italy, 1614
Faience. Biblical scenes: Joseph revealing himself to his brothers, Israelites at *seder* in Egypt, and figures of Moses, Aaron, David, and Solomon. Inscription is the text of the *kiddush* and the order of the *seder*
Courtesy, The Jewish Museum, New York City

Passover, which falls on the fifteenth of *Nissan*, the period of Israel's deliverance from Egyptian bondage, became one of the three pilgrimage festivals, when every Israelite, or his representative, went up to sacrifice at the Temple in Jerusalem. The others are *Sukkot* and *Shavuot*.

For each of these festivals marks a great day in Jewish history, while also serving as an agricultural landmark. *Sukkot* is the time for ingathering of the fruit; Passover for the early harvest, and *Shavuot* the second harvest. Each has special readings from the Bible, as well as observances applying to planting and reaping on the sacred soil.

The biblical story of Israel's liberation from their long slavery in Egypt is universally known. At first Joseph and his brethren, their families and descendants, prospered in that land. Then arose a new Pharaoh who feared lest the Israelites "grow too mighty, join Egypt's enemies," and threaten his power. He enslaved the entire people, forcing them to perform the most difficult labor. Since they still kept growing in numbers, he decreed that all Jewish boy babies be slaughtered. But the infant Moses was saved, grew up in the palace of Pharaoh's daughter, and when the time came recognized his origin and led the redemption of his people.

But Passover as a festival of human freedom is also related to the event at Mount Sinai. The Hebrews were not delivered from Egyptian bondage only that they might achieve political liberty, national independence. They were sent forth in order "that they might serve the Lord." Hence the Exodus was complete

"AND THE EGYPTIANS COMPELLED THE CHILDREN OF ISRAEL TO LABOR WITH RIGOR." *Exodus 1:13*
Copper engraving from a Bible, Holland, 1725.

WINE CUP FOR PROPHET ELIJAH
Silver, repousee work and cast
In addition to the traditional four cups of wine drunk during the *seder,* a special cup is filled with wine for the prophet Elijah, who will announce the coming of the Messiah.
Courtesy, The Jewish Museum, New York City

only when the Israelites reached Mount Sinai, and there learnt how to conduct themselves in relation to both God and man. Physical freedom alone is not sufficient; as one rabbi expressed it, "There is no free man except him who engages in the Torah." Freedom must be accompanied by law, so that men may be able best to live together. Not the mere deliverance of human beings from slavery made Israel a nation, but the giving of the Law at the festival time known as *Shavuot.*

112

The story of Passover has given inspiration to countless millions through the centuries, to break the bonds of slavery and lift their heads to the level of any man. Its influence can be traced in the liberation movements of France, America, and many other peoples that revolted to freedom. For independence is the first requisite in the proper development of humanity.

As the late Chief Rabbi Joseph H. Hertz of the British Empire expressed the thought in his Daily Prayer Book: "Passover . . commemorates an event — the redemption of Israel from Egyptian slavery—that has changed the destinies of humanity. The story of that event . . has become one of the parables of mankind; and has been a light to the Western peoples in their long and weary warfare for liberty. It taught them that God, Who in Egypt espoused the cause of brick-making slaves

PAGES FROM THE PASSOVER HAGGADAH, painted by Aaron Herlingen of Gewitsch (Moravia), 18th century. From the collections of the Bezalel Museum, Jerusalem
Courtesy, American Fund for Israel Institutions

113

against a royal oppressor, was a God of justice and freedom . . . . Thus, the most Jewish of the festivals, Israel's birthday, is as timely today as it was thousands of years ago, and has a message for men of all creeds and all races."

After a long stay away from Egypt, during which time he married the daughter of a priest of neighboring Midian and had two sons, Moses returned with his brother Aaron—to the court of Pharaoh. Pharaoh was persuaded, by way of miracles, to release his slaves, but quickly changed his mind. It took ten plagues, particularly the last, which brought about the death of all firstborn sons among the Egyptians, to assure his final consent. Even then, he sent his army after the fleeing slaves, and the soldiers drowned in the Red Sea — which had first divided to permit the Israelites to cross.

The people were unable to prepare their dough properly in escaping. The unleavened bread which they baked in the sun as they traveled is the *matzah* which the Bible compels us to eat in place of ordinary bread through all the days of the festival. The holiday is therefore known as *Hag ha-Matzot*, Feast of Unleavened Bread.

Passover observance really begins on the morning before the holiday. For all

Pages from Hagaddah, Central European, 15th century. Showing the hard labor of the Israelites in Egypt in building the two cities, Pithom and Raamses.

firstborn sons are expected to fast on that day, to memorialize the escape of the Jewish firstborn sons when the Angel of Death entered the homes of the Egyptians during the final plague. To avoid this requirement, present day oldest sons meet after morning service, and complete some sacred book, thus making the day a festive one, on which no fast may be observed.

The dietary laws are most strict in regard to Passover. The slightest amount of leaven, or souring stuff *(hametz)*, is prohibited in the home. On the previous eve, before the holiday begins, we search in all the crannies of the house for bits of this *hametz,* and it is all burnt the following morning, with suitable blessings and formulas. The greatest care is taken to purchase only food prepared according to the Passover laws. Virtually all dishes, pots, and utensils are different, and these are used on Passover only.

The great celebration of the festival is the *seder,* for the first two nights (one night only, of course, in Israel), when the *Haggadah* (narration) of Passover is read, special foods are blessed and eaten, and a veritable banquet is served. Even the least observant of adult Jews looks back upon the *seder* as the happiest occasion of life with his parents.

Outside Israel (because of the time difference) there are two days of full observance, four of partial observance *(Hol ha-Moed)*, and two more days of full festival. In Israel there are seven days in all, only the first and last of which are fully observed. On Passover, the rainy season having ended, there is a special prayer for dew. On the second night begins the counting of the Omer, the ancient measure of the winter barley offered in the Temple. This counting proceeds for forty-nine days, and culminates in the festival of *Shavuot*.

Another name for Passover is *Hag he-Aviv*, Spring Festival. It is a season of rebirth, with nature coming to life again, and the light of liberty and life spreading over the peoples. It has always been a festival of hope and gratitude for all mankind.

PASSOVER PLATE, Poland, 17th century
Brass; rampant lions support medallion inscribed, "Thus did Hillel at the time the Temple existed," from the Haggadah.

116

OMER CALENDAR IN FORM OF TORAH ARK, Holland, 18th century
Wooden case holding parchment manuscript with painted floral decorations
Omer scroll used in some synagogues for counting the 49 days between the second day of Passover and
Shavuot. "And ye shall count unto you from the morrow after the day of rest, from the day that ye
brought the sheaf of the waving; seven weeks shall there be complete; even unto the morrow after the
seventh week shall ye number fifty days." *Lev. 23:15, 16*
Courtesy, The Jewish Museum, New York City

LAG BA'OMER

The counting of the *Omer* (a measure of barley), which comprises the days between Passover and Shavuot, is one of mourning and sad memories. No feasts,
no weddings, may then be celebrated.

But the thirty-third day of this period, known as *Lag ba-Omer* (the letters
"L-g" have the Hebrew numerical value of thirty-three) is an exception. This day
is linked with three distinguished names in Jewish history—Bar Kochba, who led

117

"SAFED IN GALILEE" water color by Elias Newman
The wonderful landscape renders it the fit homeland of the lofty thoughts of poets and visionaries, and the "precious enclave" of mysticism, Kabbalah, and Hassidism.
Courtesy, Dr. Israel Goldstein, New York City.

the revolt against the Romans eighteen centuries ago, Rabbi Akiba, and Rabbi Simeon bar Yochai. For three years Bar Kochba fought on, until overwhelmed by the Roman legions. Rabbi Akiba, one of the greatest of talmudic scholars, though all of ninety years old, fought with him, as did his forty thousand disciples. A mysterious plague destroyed twenty-four thousand of these embattled students; it was lifted on the thirty-third day of the *Omer*. Rabbi Simeon, forbidden to teach the Torah, is said to have hidden in a cave for many years; on *Lag ba-Omer* he revealed to his students many secrets of the Torah.

It has been the custom for children to cease their studies on the day, and betake themselves to the open fields, in memory of these ancient events. In Israel today many make a pilgrimage to Meron, a village in Galilee, where Rabbi Simeon is buried. At midnight they kindle a bonfire and dance until dawn. The idea of bonfires and dances has spread, and now similar celebrations take place throughout the land.

118

SHAVUOT

TORAH CROWN, Poland, 1778
Silver, hammered, with bird finial
Courtesy, The Jewish Museum, New York City

Hag-ha-shavuot means the Feast of Weeks. It takes place seven weeks after the counting of the *Omer* begins on Passover. It is one of the pilgrimage festivals; and on it *bikkurim*, or first fruits, are brought to the Temple. It is also *Hag ha-Katzir*, Feast of the Harvest (wheat). That is why the synagogues today are so beautifully decorated with flowers and fruit on the holiday. *Shavuot* falls on the sixth of *Sivan*, in May or early June.

But it is primarily remembered as *Zeman Mattan Toratenu*—the Time of the Giving of Our Law. For on this day according to tradition the Torah was submitted to Israel from Mount Sinai through Moses. *Shavuot* is therefore the birthday of the Jewish religion, as Passover is the birthday of the Jewish nation.

Milk foods and honey are largely eaten on *Shavuot*. This custom is derived from the phrase in the Song of Songs, "Honey and milk shall be under your tongue" —an implication, say the sages, that the words of the Torah may be as pleasant and acceptable to our ears and hearts as are milk and honey to our tongues.

Because of its relationship to the Torah, *Shavuot* has long been an acceptable time for a child to begin his religious studies. Many men spend the entire first night in studying *Tikkun Shavuot*. The latter is an anthology from the Bible, Talmud, the mystic Zohar, and many other sacred volumes. A long poem by Rabbi Meir ben Isaac of Orleans, who lived in the eleventh century, is recited with a special chant before the synagogue reading from the Torah during the morning services; this poem, called *Akdamut*, praises the Jewish people for their attachment to their Creator and to His Law.

The special reading for *Shavuot* is the Book of Ruth. For in telling the story of this ancestor of King David, and her acceptance of Israel's religion, the Bible gives an account of the grain harvest, and of how the poor were aided during the reaping. There is also a tradition, found in the Talmud, that David was born and died on *Shavuot*.

On Passover we are commanded to assume that we ourselves are participating in the Exodus from Egypt and are being freed from bondage. On *Shavuot* it is brought home to us that the Torah given on Mount Sinai was also given to us; we accept it anew and once again dedicate ourselves to its glorious teachings.

"FEAST OF WEEKS" (SHAVUOT) by Moritz Oppenheim (1880-1882), Germany
"And thou shalt keep the feast of weeks unto the Lord thy God . . . and thou shalt rejoice before the Lord thy God . . ." *Deut. 16:10, 11*
Courtesy, Oscar Gruss, New York City

"How were the first fruits brought? Those who lived near Jerusalem brought fresh figs and grapes, and those who lived far away brought dried figs and raisins. In front of them went an ox, its horns overlaid with gold and a wreath of olive leaves on its head.

"The flute played before them until they reached Jerusalem. They then sent messengers and decorated their first fruits. The rulers, the chief priests, and the treasurers of the Temple went out to meet them; and all the craftsmen of Jerusalem stood up and greeted them with the words, 'Brethren, ye are welcome!' (Talmud)

And when ye reap the harvest of your land, thou shalt not wholly reap the corner of thy field . . . .
And thou shalt not glean thy vineyard . . . Thou shalt leave them for the poor and for the strangers . . . .   Lev. 19:9-10

"RUTH" by E. M. Lilien, (1874-1925)
"And she gleaned in the field after the reapers"

בִּימֵי שְׁפֹט הַשּׁפְטִים וַיְהִי רָעָב בָּאָרֶץ וַיֵּלֶךְ

אִישׁ מִבֵּית לֶחֶם יְהוּדָה לָגוּר בִּשְׂדֵי מוֹאָב הוּא

אִשְׁתּוֹ וּשְׁנֵי בָנָיו : וְשֵׁם הָאִישׁ אֱלִימֶלֶךְ וְשֵׁם אִשְׁתּוֹ נָעֳמִי וְשֵׁם

שְׁנֵי בָנָיו מַחְלוֹן וְכִלְיוֹן אֶפְרָתִים מִבֵּית לֶחֶם יְהוּדָה וַיָּבֹאוּ שְׂדֵי

מוֹאָב וַיִּהְיוּ שָׁם : וַיָּמָת אֱלִימֶלֶךְ אִישׁ נָעֳמִי וַתִּשָּׁאֵר הִיא וּשְׁנֵי

בָנֶיהָ : וַיִּשְׂאוּ לָהֶם נָשִׁים מֹאֲבִיּוֹת שֵׁם הָאַחַת עָרְפָּה וְשֵׁם

PAGE SHOWING THE HARVEST ACCORDING TO THE BOOK OF RUTH, Italy, early 18th century
Courtesy, The Library of The Jewish Theological Seminary of America, New York City

THE WRITTEN LAW

A Bible Published by the Jerusalem Bible Publishing Company

BIBLE — TANAKH
The Hebrew Bible consists of twenty-four books grouped into three divisions: (a) *Torah* — the Law or Five Books of Moses; (b) *Nebiim* — the Prophets; and (c) *Ketubim* — Hagiographa or Holy Writings. From the initial letters of the Hebrew names for the three divisions we get the commonly used word for the Bible, *Tanakh.*

"And these words, which I command thee this day, shall be upon thy heart; and thou shalt teach them diligently unto thy children . . . . " Deut. 6:6-7

This book of the law shall not depart out of thy mouth, but thou shalt meditate therein day and night, that thou mayest observe to do according to all that is written therein; for then thou shalt make thy ways prosperous, and then thou shalt have good success. *Josh. 1:8*

THE ORAL LAW

מאימתי

מאימתי קורין את שמע בערבין. משעה שהכהנים נכנסים לאכול בתרומתן, עד סוף האשמורה הראשונה, דברי רבי אליעזר. וחכמים אומרים עד חצות. רבן גמליאל אומר עד שיעלה עמוד השחר. מעשה ובאו בניו מבית המשתה, אמרו לו לא קרינו את שמע, אמר להם אם לא עלה עמוד השחר חייבין אתם לקרות. ולא זו בלבד אמרו, אלא כל מה שאמרו חכמים עד חצות מצותן עד שיעלה עמוד השחר. הקטר חלבים ואברים מצותן עד שיעלה עמוד השחר, וכל הנאכלים ליום אחד מצותן עד שיעלה עמוד השחר. אם כן למה אמרו חכמים עד חצות, כדי להרחיק אדם מן העבירה:

גמ׳ תנא היכא קאי דקתני מאימתי. ותו מאי שנא דתני בערבית ברישא, לתני דשחרית ברישא. תנא אקרא קאי דכתיב בשכבך ובקומך, והכי קתני זמן קריאת שמע דשכיבה אימת, משעה שהכהנים נכנסים לאכול בתרומתן. ואי בעית אימא יליף מברייתו של עולם דכתיב ויהי ערב ויהי בקר יום אחד. אי הכי סיפא דקתני בשחר מברך שתים לפניה ואחת לאחריה, ובערב מברך שתי לפניה ושתי לאחריה, לתני דערבית ברישא בשחרית. תנא פתח בערבית והדר תני בשחרית, עד דקאי בשחרית פריש מילי דשחרית והדר פריש מילי דערבית.

אמר מר משעה שהכהנים נכנסים לאכול בתרומתן, מכדי כהנים אימת קא אכלי תרומה משעת צאת הכוכבים, לתני משעת צאת הכוכבים. מלתא אגב אורחיה קמשמע לן כהנים אימת קא אכלי בתרומה משעת צאת הכוכבים, והא קמ״ל דכפרה לא מעכבא כדתניא ובא השמש וטהר, ביאת שמשו מעכבתו מלאכול בתרומה ואין כפרתו מעכבתו מלאכול בתרומה. וממאי דהאי ובא השמש ביאת השמש והאי וטהר טהר יומא דילמא.

FIRST PAGE OF THE FIRST VOLUME OF THE TALMUD, CALLED BERAKHOT

Center text: The Mishnah and Gemara, the code of Jewish law and rabbinic discussions thereof. Surrounding text: Commentaries of *Rashi* (1040-1105), the *Tosaphot,* and others.

"THE WAILING WALL" oil by D. Bida
"How doth the city sit solitary, that was full of people . . . from the daughter of Zion all her beauty is departed." *Lamentations*
Courtesy, The Jewish Museum, New York City

TISHAH B'AV

Tishah B'Av, the ninth day of the month Av (or Ab), is an extraordinary date in Jewish history.

On that day, says the Talmud, occurred these fearful events: "The decree that Israel should wander through the wilderness for forty years; the destruction of the First Temple by Nebuchadnezzar (586 before the common era), and of the Second Temple by Titus (in the year 70); fall of the fortress of Bethar (135); the subsequent defeat of Bar Kochba and massacre of his men; and the plowing up of Jerusalem (under Hadrian, 135)."

126

But there were later calamities on the ninth of Av. It was on this day, in 1290, that Edward I signed the edict expelling the Jews from England; and in 1492, 300,000 Jews, led by Abarbanel, began their departure from the Spain of Ferdinand and Isabella. The Jews of Spain had lived there in peace for centuries, and enriched the country materially as well as in literature and scholarship. They could no longer endure the fear and tortures of the Inquisition. Most of them were expelled, perished from hunger, drowned, or were sold into slavery.

To our sages, the greatest of all calamities was that which first sent the Jewish people into exile. To mourn the destruction of the temples, Jews were commanded to abstain from food and labor on the ninth of Av. It is said that all who thus mourn for Jerusalem will witness the restoration of its ancient glory — which seems to mean that only by mourning our loss through the ages, and commemorating our past greatness, could we hope to seek to retrieve the Holy City of our past. This prophecy is being realized today, through the merit of those who for so long fasted and wept on the day of destruction. Recall of the past has been the major factor in recognizing our unity, our continuity, and our destiny.

Prayer shawl and phylacteries are not worn at early services, to show our mourning. Instead they are donned for the afternoon prayer. In announcing the coming of the Hebrew month we call it *Menahem Av*, "menahem" meaning comforter. Hope has sprung eternally among the exiled people of Israel.

Observant Jews doff their shoes and seat themselves on the floor when they begin the services in the synagogue. The Lamentations of Jeremiah are mournfully chanted, both in the evening and the morning, generally by dim lights. *Ekhah*, Hebrew name of Lamentations, is the first word of the book. No sadder elegy has ever been written. *Kinnot*, dirges, are recited through the day. Yet in all of these, particularly the odes composed by Judah Halevi, the hope of a restored Zion is never lacking.

MODEL OF KING SOLOMON'S TEMPLE, built by Joseph Doctorowitz.
Based on text from the Bible.
Courtesy, The Jewish Museum. New York City

SPECIAL CEREMONY ON TISHAH B'AV IN KING DAVID'S TOMB ON MT. ZION, JERUSALEM
Crowns are removed from their resting place for this day of mourning.
Courtesy, New York University J.C.F. Library of Judaica.

For it has been the immemorial tradition in Jewry that at the very moment God punishes His people he prepares for their healing. Our ancestors believed that on the day the Temple was destroyed occurred the birth of the Messiah. And each year, on the Sabbath following Tishah B'Av — called *Shabbat Nahamu* — we read the fortieth chapter of Isaiah, one of the most beautiful visions in all literature:

> Comfort ye, comfort ye, My people,
> Saith your God.
> Bid Jerusalem take heart,
> And proclaim unto her,
> That her time of service is accomplished,
> That her guilt is paid off;
> That she hath received of the Lord's hand
> Double for all her sins.

"DESTRUCTION OF JERUSALEM" oil by Bernard Picart (1712)

LAMENTATIONS

How doth the city sit solitary,
That was full of people!
How is she become as a widow!
She that was great among the nations,
And princess among the provinces,
How is she become tributary!
She weepeth sore in the night,
And her tears are on her cheeks;
She hath none to comfort her
Among all her lovers;
All her friends have dealt treacherously with her,
They are become her enemies.

Lam. 1: 1-2

The ways of Zion do mourn,
Because none come to the solemn assembly;
All her gates are desolate,
Her priests sigh;
Her virgins are afflicted,
And she herself is in bitterness.

Lam. 1: 4

And gone is from the daughter of Zion
All her splendour;
Her princes are become like harts
That find no pasture,
And they are gone without strength
Before the pursuer.
Jerusalem remembereth
In the days of her afflication and of her anguish
All her treasures that she had
From the days of old;
Now that her people fall by the hand of the adversary,
And none doth help her,
The adversaries have seen her,
They have mocked at her desolations.

Lam. 1: 6-7

For these things I weep;
Mine eye, mine eye runneth down with water;
Because the comforter is far from me,
Even he that should refresh my soul;
My children are desolate,
Because the enemy hath prevailed.

Lam. 1: 16

I called for my lovers,
But they deceived me;
My priests and mine elders
Perished in the city,
While they sought them food
To refresh their souls.
Behold, O Lord, for I am in distress,
Mine inwards burn;
My heart is turned within me,
For I have grievously rebelled.
Abroad the sword bereaveth,
At home there is the like of death.

Lam. 1: 19-20

Arise, cry out in the night,
At the beginning of the watches;
Pour out thy heart like water
Before the face of the Lord;
Lift up thy hands toward Him
For the life of thy young children,
That faint for hunger
At the head of every street.

Lam. 2: 19

"JEREMIAH," by E. M. Lilien (1874-1925)

I am the man that hath seen affliction
By the rod of His wrath.
He hath led me and caused me to walk
In darkness and not in light.

Lam. 3: 1-2

How is the gold become dim!
How is the most fine gold changed!
The hallowed stones are poured out
At the head of every street!
The precious sons of Zion,
Comparable to fine gold,
How are they esteemed as earthen pitchers,
The work of the hands of the potter!
Even the jackals draw out the breast,
They give suck to their young ones;
The daughter of my people is become cruel,
Like the ostriches in the wilderness.

Lam. 4: 1-3

Remember, O Lord, what is come upon us;
Behold, and see our reproach.
Our inheritance is turned unto strangers,
Our houses unto aliens.
We are become orphans and fatherless,
Our mothers are as widows.
We have drunk our water for money;
Our wood cometh to us for price.
To our very necks we are pursued;
We labour, and have no rest.

Lam. 5: 1-5

Turn thou us unto Thee, O Lord,
and we shall be turned;
Renew our days as of old.

Lam. 5: 21

130

Menorah designed at New Bezalel Arts and Crafts School, Jerusalem
Courtesy, American Fund for Israel Institutions.

OTHER FASTS

There are also other fast days in Judaism, observed from sunrise rather than from the previous evening, as is the case with *Yom Kippur* and *Tish'ah B'Av.* Some pious Jews, in search of repentance, fast a cycle of Monday, Thursday, and Monday, after Passover or *Sukkot.* Fasts as a means of beseeching God for help and victory, are frequently mentioned in the Bible. Communities have often fasted in times of distress. During the Hitler persecutions rabbis throughout the world also ordained fasts of supplication.

On the seventeenth of *Tammuz* the walls of Jerusalem were breached, leading to destruction of the Second Temple in 70 A.D. The Talmud records other misfortunes that took place on that day, such as: the tablets of the Ten Commandments were broken; and the daily Temple offerings ceased during the siege of Jerusalem, for lack of animals. Three weeks after the seventeenth of *Tammuz* is the ninth of Av, when the first destruction took place.

There is also *Tzom Gedaliah,* the fast decreed for the day after *Rosh Hashanah* because of the murder on that day of Gedaliah, governor appointed by Nebuchadnezzar, which brought fearful retaliation upon the people. Another fast falls on the tenth of *Tevet,* when Nebuchadnezzar began his siege.

But it must be remembered that on the whole, despite all these evidences, Judaism does not favor excess of self-mortification.

THE SYNAGOGUE

For nearly twenty-five hundred years the synagogue has been the fortress of the Jewish spirit. When the First Temple was destroyed in 586 B.C.E., and our forefathers were exiled to Babylonia, they would gather there to read passages from the Torah and the Prophets, to recall the Temple ceremonies, and to observe the fast and feast days. These meetings were called *knesset,* gathering. First they met in private homes. When they erected permanent houses of worship, each became a *Bet Knesset* — house of meeting. The Greek word *synagogue* has the same meaning.

The Jews who returned from Babylonian exile in 536 B.C.E. rebuilt the Temple. But everywhere outside the Land they continued building synagogues. Philo, first century phil-

INTERIOR OF PORTUGUESE SYNAGOGUE, AMSTERDAM. Dedicated 1675.

RUINS OF ANCIENT SYNAGOGUE AT KFAR BIRAM

BETH ALPHA SYNAGOGUE, part of the large mosaic floor from this 6th century synagogue, discovered when Jewish pioneer settlers were digging trenches for foundation walls of a new building.

osopher of Alexandria, Egypt, wrote: "On the seventh day the Jews stop all work and proceed to sacred spots which they call synagogues. There, arranged in rows according to their ages, the younger below the older, they sit quietly as befits the occasion, with attentive ears. Then one of them takes the book, and reads aloud to the others . . . "

After destruction of the Second Temple in the year 70, the synagogue acquired many new functions. It became both house of worship, center of study, and focal point for the community. Here religious leaders addressed the people; wayfarers came for help and hospitality; and emissaries from the Holy Land or other communities sought assistance. In addition to *Bet Knesset,* the synagogue was called *Bet Am,* house of the people; *Bet Tefillah,* house of prayer; and *Bet Midrash,* house of study.

In countries of oppression, building synagogues was often prohibited, or their height was kept below that of churches or mosques. But in ancient Alexandria the synagogue was large and imposing. Excavations in Syria and Palestine have uncovered remains of richly adorned Jewish houses of worship in Dura Europe, Capernaum, Beth Alpha, and many other sites.

Despite a great variety of arch-

TORAH ARK IN THE SYNAGOGUE OF ARI, OLDEST SYNAGOGUE IN SAFED, ISRAEL

"SYNAGOGUE OF VILNA, POLAND" by Marc Chagall
Courtesy, M. Cottin, Lakewood, New Jersey

itecture, synagogue buildings have clung to certain rules in construction. The most important feature has always been the Holy Ark, or *Aron ha-kodesh,* set in a wall recess to face the congregation. This permanent receptacle for the Scrolls of the Law is named after the *Aron ha-Berit,* or Ark of the Convenant, which held the Ten Commandments when the early Israelites traversed the desert. As a rule the Ark is built in the east wall, so that the worshipers may face east as they pray.

Above the Ark there are representations of the Tables of the Law, and other decorations, such as rampant lions of Judah. As the children of Israel, in their wanderings,

136

INTERIOR OF SYNAGOGUE HURVAH
One of the oldest synagogues in Old
Jerusalem, destroyed by the Arabs in 1948

hung a curtain before the Ark, synagogues today employ the highly ornate, embroidered *parokhet,* made of satin or velvet, to embellish their own Arks. There may be a short hanging also, called *kapporet,* emulating the long descriptions of the sacred object in the Book of Exodus.

The *Ner Tamid,* Eternal Light, gleams perpetually before every synagogue Ark. It is a symbol of God's presence among His creatures. In Temple days the lamp that was never extinguished was fed with pure olive oil. Today electric bulbs serve the same purpose in most American synagogues.

The *bimah,* or reading platform, where the assigned portions from the Torah and the Prophets are recited, is an elevated structure found just before the Ark. In all Sephardic structures, and most Ashkenazic synagogues completely traditional, the *bimah* is placed in the center of the house of worship. This is reminiscent of the middle compartment of the Temple, where in ancient days stood altar, table, and candelabrum.

137

INTERIOR VIEW OF MODERN YESHURUN SYNAGOGUE IN JERUSALEM, showing the platform and the Torah Ark

The large seven-branched candelabrum, as prescribed by Exodus, is found in many fine metals and designs in all congregations. The reading desk is covered by embroidered fabrics. It has been the custom for Jews to donate the several articles of furniture and their coverings in honor of deceased relatives; thus they may bear not alone sacred inscriptions, but also the names of those memorialized.

The synagogue has always been used for discourses by the spiritual leader or a visiting preacher as well as for prayer. The prayers were varied as to content and phraseology, and in early centuries full freedom for such variations was permitted readers and worshipers. In the ninth century, Rab Amram for the first time — so far as extant manuscripts show — established a permanent order of prayers. Since that time prayerbooks for every day, the Sabbath, and the festivals, as well as the high holidays, have been produced, until in these days there are standard liturgies for all purposes, published in many forms but all based upon the accepted prayers and blessings employed for many generations.

It must never be forgotten that the synagogue was at no time a mere meeting place for prayer quorums *(minyanim)*. Judaism did not, and does not, look upon

TOURO SYNAGOGUE, Newport, Rhode Island
The oldest synagogue building in the United States, dedicated in 1763 (congregation founded 1658)

repetition of prescribed orisons as its sole purpose. It has always been the school house (the common word "schul" applied to traditional synagogues is really the German word for school). Also it has served as Bet *haMidrash,* the academy for more advanced students, and for mature men who wish to study Talmud and other sacred volumes between services or at other available seasons.

139

Special service in 1954 at Manhattan's Congregation Shearith Israel, oldest Jewish congregation in the United States, inaugurating the celebration of the anniversary of three hundred years of American Jewish life.
Courtesy, Congregation Shearith Israel, New York City

In the synagogue too, weddings were celebrated; and from it funerals of important and learned men were conducted. Public announcements of importance were made from the *bimah;* it was permitted on Sabbath for petitioners seeking redress from wrongs to interrupt the reading service to address the congregation. When rabbinical courts sought to enforce their decrees, they did so through the forum afforded by the synagogue platform.

The *schul* has perennially served as the center of philanthropy. A poor box was suspended near the door, for all to see. From its receipts local poor and indigent transients were cared for. There was a charity chest *(kuppah)* to provide a fuller quota of funds to assist the town charities. In many towns travelers slept in the synagogue, and ate their Sabbath meal there. For this reason there developed the custom of reciting the *kiddush* at synagogue services, for the benefit of strangers who would not hear this benediction at home. On Passover, when strangers are brought into the homes of local householders, the *kiddush* is not recited in the holy place.

A notable recent occurrence in America is the dynamic interest in the construction of synagogues and temples, with much care and attention focused on architectural design and beauty of ornamentation. Following are examples of modern design applied to houses of worship representing orthodox, conservative, and reform Judaism.

TAYLOR ROAD SYNAGOGUE, CLEVELAND HEIGHTS, OHIO. (ORTHODOX)

Milo S. Holdstein, A.I.A., Architect
Albert Strom, Interior Design

TEMPLE EMETH, CHESTNUT HILL, MASS.
(CONSERVATIVE)

Photographs by Samuel Cooper

TEMPLE BETH SHOLOM, MIAMI BEACH, FLORIDA (REFORM)

"THE MIRACLE" by Jacques Lipchitz
Bronze
Courtesy, The Jewish Museum, New York City

EIGHT CLASSES OF CHARITY

Maimonides divided the dispensers of charity (*zedakah*) into **eight classes** according to rising degrees of merit:

1. Those who bestow charity but complainingly.
2. Those who do so cheerfully but give less than they should.
3. Those who contribute only when they are asked and the sum they are asked.
4. Those who give before they are requested to.
5. Those who give charity but do not know who benefits by it, although the recipient is aware from whom he has received it.
6. Those who give charity and do not disclose their names to those who have received it.
7. Those who do not know to whom their contribution will be given, while the recipients do not know from whom they have received it.
8. Those who extend a loan or bestow a gift upon the needy, or who take a poor man into partnership, or help him to establish himself in business, so that he should not be compelled to apply for charity. Such people practice the highest degree of charity.

SEAL DESIGNED BY THOMAS JEFFERSON
Taken from the Exodus, depicts Pharaoh engulfed in the Red Sea
Proposed by Jefferson, Franklin, and Adams as official seal of the United States in 1776
Courtesy, G. P. Putnam and Sons, New York City

JUDAISM AND AMERICAN IDEALS
by Abraham I. Katsh

Judaism and American democracy have much in common. Both teach the unity of the human race. Both have their foundation in "Love thy neighbor as thyself." Both are motivated by moral considerations. Both aim to create, to build, to contribute, and to share. Both regard the the divine character of human personality. Both command respect for the religious convictions of others, and the practice of charity toward all. Both aim toward walking humbly with God and in modesty among men. Both emphasize the conscientious observance of the laws of the state, respect for and obedience to the government. Both are based upon the natural right of a person to be different and not to be penalized for the difference. Both stand for a government by the consent of the governed. Both recognize the fact that material and spiritual benefits of society belong to the whole of society and that the focal point of social process is in the individual and not in the state.

The Puritans in America actually thought of themselves as a new Israel, fighting wickedness and paganism to exterminate those who were on the side of Satan. Their lot became the lot of Israel. If Egypt had been to Israel a "land of bondage," so was England to the Puritans. Like the Israelites they memorialized, in the scriptural text, their plight. On the title page of the first edition of "New England's Memorial" appears the biblical text: ". . . and thou shalt remember all the way which the Lord thy God led thee this forty years in the wilderness."

In searching the Scriptures for a text relevant to their own particular needs the Puritans soon discovered the general similarity between themselves and the ancient Israelites. They firmly believed that the Hebrew prophets spoke to them as directly as they had spoken to the Hebrews. The life of the Israelites as related in the Bible served them as a mirror in which they could see reflected their own activities.

145

Comparisons of Puritan leaders with Moses and Joshua were very common. For example, in Cotton Mather's *Magnalia Christi Americana* we find the following in regard to John Winthrop of the Massachusetts colony: "Accordingly when the noble design of carrying a colony of chosen people into an American wilderness, was by some eminent person undertaken, this eminent person was, by the consent of all, chosen for the Moses, who must be the leader of so great an undertaking; and indeed nothing but a Mosaic spirit could have carried him through the temptations to which either his farewell to his own land, or his travel in a strange land, must needs expose a gentleman of his education."

William Bradford too was often called Joshua. Similarly after his death, when Thomas Prince was chosen governor of New Plymouth, it was said of him: "At such a time and when the condition of this colony was such as hath been declared, God was pleased to mind it, even in its low estate, and when He had taken unto himself not only our Moses, but many of the elders and worthies of our Israel, He hath not hitherto left us without a Joshua, to lead us in the remaining of our Pilgrimage."

Names of colonies, cities, and settlements were likewise chosen from Hebraic Scripture. The names Salem (peace), Bethlehem (house of bread), and others will bear witness. The name Nahumkek, given, according to Cotton Mather, to a plantation settlement in 1628, was not, as is generally believed, of Indian but rather of Hebrew origin. The name, argued Mather, is composed of two Hebrew words: Nahum (comfort, or console) and Kek (Heq — a haven). "And our English not only found in it an Haven of Comfort, but happened also to put an Hebrew name upon it; for they called it Salem, for the peace which they had and hoped for; and so it was called unto this day."

Colonial America turned to the Old Testament for its political ideas and governmental procedure. There it found the inspiration justifying its antagonism to the principle of divine right of kings. Samuel's abhorrence of the monarchy was often the justification of the clergy in advocating separation of the colonies from England. Jona-

University Seals with Hebraic Inscriptions of Columbia and Dartmouth
Courtesy of Columbia University and Dartmouth College

146

ARMS OF YALE UNIVERSITY, WITH HEBRAIC INSCRIPTION
Courtesy, Yale University, New Haven, Connecticut

than Mayhew, a leading clergyman, frequently referred to as the father of civil and religious liberty in America, in a sermon delivered in Boston, May 23, 1766 on the repeal of the Stamp Act, declared: "God gave Israel a king (or absolute monarchy) in His anger, because they had not the sense and virtue enough to like a free commonwealth, and to have Himself for their king — where the spirit of the Lord is, there is liberty — and if any miserable people on the continent or isles of Europe be driven in their extremity to seek a safe retreat from slavery in some far distant clime — oh, let them find one in America." On these principles Mayhew fought not to table the idea of a pure democracy.

It becomes clear that Moses' warning and Samuel's admonition against monarchy actuated the policy of our United States, at the crossroads of colonial life during the third quarter of the eighteenth century. Hebraic idealism spurred our fathers to challenge monarchy and persuaded them to offer their blood in the Revolutionary War.

Of striking interest is the draft for the seal of the new United States which Franklin and Jefferson submitted. It portrayed Pharaoh, with a crown on his head and a sword in his hand, sitting in an open chariot, passing through the divided waters of the Red Sea in pursuit of the Israelites, and Moses, beams of light projecting from his face, standing on the shore and extending his hand over the sea, causing it to overwhelm Pharaoh. Underneath was the motto from the book of Maccabees: "Rebellion to tyrants is obedience to God."

There was a sufficiently widespread interest and knowledge of Hebrew in the Colonies at the time of the Revolution to allow for the circulation of a story that certain members of Congress proposed that the use of English be formally prohibited in the United States, and Hebrew substituted for it.

The spirit embodied in the Scriptures found expression in other ways. Inscribed on the Liberty Bell is the biblical verse: "Proclaim liberty throughout the land unto all the inhabitants thereof" (Lev. 25:10)—a motto which has been one of the pillars — if not the main pillar — of our constitutional democracy. Yale University immortalized the Hebrew expression "Urim V'Tummin" as its theological and educational emblem, commemorating the decorative and ceremonial breastplate worn by the High Priest during special occasions of sacrificial services. Columbia University has chosen the Tetragrammatan as its emblem. So did Dartmouth University, an institution organized to train missionaries to Indians. Hebrew inscriptions are also engraved on the walls of Yale and New York University libraries.

ראשית חכמה יראת יהוה

THE LIBERTY BELL IN INDEPENDENCE HALL, PHILADELPHIA, PA.
Cast in England in 1751, placed in Independence Hall tower in 1753.

"AND PROCLAIM

LIBERTY THROUGHOUT

THE LAND . . ."

Lev. 10:25

For three hundred years Jews have lived in America. With all other Americans, they have helped make this country great and free. They are free and equal citizens, sharing the same rights and responsibilities. The history of the country is also the history of its Jews.

Less than three and a half centuries ago the Pilgrims established their settlement in New England. Independence was achieved less than two centuries ago. The newcomers hewed out their homes from the wilderness. The Thanksgiving Day celebration, established in the early days, and each year proclaimed by the President, is reminiscent of the days when Israel dwelt in booths; it is said to have been modeled after the *Sukkot* festival.

The Declaration of Independence, signed July 4, 1776, enunciated the principle of human equality, and established the unalienable rights to life, liberty, and the pursuit of happiness. It readily brings to mind the Jewish holiday of liberation, the Passover.

"With the sweat of thy brow shalt thou eat bread." The Bible long ago expounded the dignity of labor. In keeping with this concept, once a year a day is set aside in this country to honor American labor.

Jews recall many wars, and countless sacrifices to enemy assault. They can best appreciate the sentiments of America's Memorial Day.

George Washington's Birthday reminds us of a life lived according to basic biblical principles. Lincoln, like the Israelites, sought brotherhood among men, and fought the enslavement of one man by another.

The Hebraic mortar that cemented American ideals is fully evident in the holidays we celebrate as part of the American people.

LOVE OF ZION

by Shlomo Katz

"And the Lord appeared unto Abram, and said: 'Unto thy seed will I give this land'; and he builded there an altar unto the Lord, who appeared unto him."   Gen. 12:7

The love of the Jewish people for Zion is one of the greatest stories in history. Every person loves his home, and every nation loves its country, but Jewish attachment to Eretz Israel has proven the most enduring of all. Jews have lived in many countries, but even in faraway lands they have longed for the restoration of Zion.

The patriarch Jacob, one of the three "fathers" of the Jewish people, died in Egypt, where he and his entire family had settled when famine ravaged Canaan. Before he died, Jacob called his son Joseph, viceroy of Egypt, second only to Pharaoh in authority and made him swear that he would take his father's body back to his native land. Joseph kept that promise. And when Joseph grew old and knew he had not much longer to live, he called his brothers and made them promise that when their deliverance came, they would take his bones back with them. When the Jews left Egypt in great haste hundreds of years later, they did not forget their promise.

And I will rejoice in Jerusalem,
And joy in My people;
And the voice of weeping shall be no more heard in her,
Nor the voice of crying.

ISAIAH: 65, 19

Many centuries later, a great calamity befell the people of Judah. Nebuchadnezzar, Emporer of Babylonia, conquered the land, destroyed Jerusalem, and exiled its people. Mournfully the exiles trudged the dusty desert roads on the way to Babylonia. They felt keenly the loss of their country and their capital city. As they sat weeping by the banks of a river in Babylonia, they pronouced the most solemn oath ever uttered by man: "If I forget thee, O Jerusalem, let my right hand forget her cunning. Let my tongue cleave to the roof of my mouth, if I remember thee not; if I set not Jerusalem above my chiefest joy!"

(Psalms 137: 5-6)

At the first opportunity many thousands of Jews returned, and rebuilt Jerusalem and the Temple. They loved Zion, and three times a year made their pilgrimages to Jerusalem. Even Jews in distant countries took these pilgrimages when they could, at a time when travel was difficult and dangerous.

Centuries passed. (If one wishes to understand the history and nature of the Jews, one must always remember how far back that history extends.) Once more calamity struck. The Romans destroyed Jerusalem and scattered the Jews. For almost two thousand years the Jews mourned their loss. Everywhere they observed a period of mourning on the anniversary of the destruction, the beginning of their dispersion.

The loss of Zion and the remembrance of Jerusalem were noted even on happy occasions. Until very recently, Jews in Eastern Europe would leave unpainted a small area on one of their walls to remind them that Jerusalem had been destroyed and the Jewish nation driven out of Zion. At weddings, when the bride and groom stand under the *huppah* (canopy), a glass is broken by the bridegroom as a symbolic reminder of the destruction.

Throughout the centuries Jews not only mourned for Zion; many also tried to return. The sages of olden times declared that one who lived in Eretz Israel was assured of life thereafter. They maintained that the very air of Eretz Israel makes one wise.

In the eleventh century, Judah Halevi, greatest Hebrew poet since the prophets, left his prosperous home and family in Spain, drawn by his great love for Zion. Legend tells us that when he landed in Jaffa, he prostrated himself on the sacred soil and kissed it, and as he did so, a *bedouin* rode up and killed him with his spear.

In the sixteenth century Don Joseph Nasi, a Jewish nobleman in the court of the Sultan of Turkey, obtained permission for Jews to settle in Tiberias, and many flocked there. Others settled in Jerusalem, in Safed, and in other cities, though Jerusalem in particular attracted them because it was the site of the Temple, and there they could come to the Western Wall (the only part of the Temple still standing), commonly referred to as the "Wailing Wall," — to pray and to voice their grief. In the middle of the eighteenth century, a considerable number of pious Jews went to Palestine from Eastern Europe. Some were disciples of the *Gaon* Elijah of Vilna; others were adherents of the newly-established *hassidic* movement. In Palestine they settled in the "Four Holy Cities" — Jerusalem, Hebron, Safed, Tiberias.

But the great return to Zion began about seventy years ago. A group of young Jews in Russia organized themselves into a group called *BILU*. This name is made of the initials of the Hebrew words *Bet Yaacov Lekhu Venelkha*—"House of Jacob, come, and let us go." In Palestine they set up the first modern Jewish agricultural settlements. They were followed by a wave of young pioneers imbued with the desire to build in Eretz Israel a new Jewish society. Succeeding waves of immigration brought hundreds of thousands; and in 1948 they won independence for the

Perfect in beauty, Zion, how in thee
Do love and grace unite!
The souls of thy companions tenderly
Turn unto thee; thy joy was their delight,
And, weeping, they lament thy ruin now.
In distant exile, for thy sacred height
They long, and towards thy gates in prayer they bow.
The Lord desires thee for his dwelling-place
Eternally; and blest
Is he whom God has chosen for the grace
Within thy courts to rest.
Happy is he that watches, drawing near,
Until he sees thy glorious light arise,
And over whom thy dawn breaks full and clear
Set in the orient skies.
But happiest he, who, with exultant eyes,
The bliss of thy redeemed ones shall behold.
And see thy youth renewed as in the days of old.

—From "ODE TO ZION," *Jehuda Halevi* (1086-1145)

MOUNT ZION

Bnei Brak, near Tel Aviv

new State of Israel.

Since 1948, additional hundreds of thousands have migrated to Israel. When they arrive, many emulate the example of Judah Halevi, bending down and kissing the soil of the land which they and their forefathers so long yearned for. Countless thousands of others in Europe, Asia, and Africa are hoping for the day when they too will be able to return to Zion. Jews of America, also cherishing great love for the land, help in the rebuilding of modern Zion, the historic home of the Jewish people.

Exhibit of Hebrew and English books of Jewish interest and a variety of modern Hebrew and Anglo-Jewish periodicals.

Library, Baltimore Hebrew College
Baltimore, Maryland

For centuries Hebrew was confined chiefly to the religious sphere. Spoken Hebrew was still a dream only a hundred years ago, although modern Hebrew appeared in Italy about two centuries ago. The great literary heritage — Bible, Talmud, Midrashim, medieval philosophy and poetry — which had nourished the Jewish spirit, is now presented in such a manner as to keep its hold upon the new Hebrew speaking generation growing up in Israel and Jewish communities throughout the world.

152

Menorah designed by A. Raymond Katz
Temple Israel, Canton, Ohio

A Psalm of David.

Lord, who shall sojourn in Thy tabernacle?
Who shall dwell upon Thy holy mountain?
He that walketh uprightly, and worketh righteousness,
And speaketh truth in his heart;
That hath no slander upon his tongue,
Nor doeth evil to his fellow,
Nor taketh up a reproach against his neighbor;
In whose eyes a vile person is despised,
But he honoureth them that fear the Lord;
He that sweareth to his own hurt, and changeth not;
He that putteth not out his money on interest,
Nor taketh a bribe against the innocent,
He that doeth these things shall never be moved.

Psalm 15

And the spirit of the Lord shall rest upon him,
The spirit of wisdom and understanding,
The spirit of counsel and might,
The spirit of knowledge and of the fear of the Lord.
And his delight shall be in the fear of the Lord;
And he shall not judge after the sight of his eyes,
Neither decide after the hearing of his ears;
But with righteousness shall he judge the poor,
And decide with equity for the meek of the land;
And he shall smite the land with the rod of his mouth,
And with the breath of his lips shall he slay the wicked.
And righteousness shall be the girdle of his loins,
And faithfulness the girdle of his reins.
And the wolf shall dwell with the lamb,
And the leopard shall lie down with the kid;
And the calf and the young lion and the fatling together;
And a little child shall lead them.
And the cow and the bear shall feed;
Their young ones shall lie down together;
And the lion shall eat straw like the ox.
And the suckling child shall play on the hole of the asp,
And the weaned child shall put his hand on the basilisk's den.
They shall not hurt nor destroy
In all My holy mountain;
For the earth shall be full of the knowledge of the Lord,
As the waters cover the sea.

Isaiah, 11:2-10

154

THE TWELVE TRIBES, EMANATING FROM THE INITIALS OF THE FATHERS, Mosaic by A. Raymond Katz, made for Beth Yehuda Synagogue, Lock Haven, Pennsylvania.

HIGHLIGHTS OF THE HISTORY OF THE JEWS

by Meyer Waxman

The Jews Become a Nation

The history of the Jewish people differs in many respects from those of other nations. Jewish history extends far into the past, whereas most nations are of relatively recent origin. It also encompasses nearly the entire earth, for Jewish communities have existed in almost every country of the world at one time or another. Because of its large extent in time and space, the Jewish story is marked by a multitude of important events which reflect the history of all humanity.

The history of the Jews as a nation began in the Sinai Desert, when the Israelites, who had just been liberated from the bondage of Egypt, received the Torah on Mt. Sinai. The Torah is, in effect, the Jewish constitution. It provides both the laws to be observed and the ideals to be attained. By means of these laws and ideals, the mass of former slaves were unified and made distinct from the other nations of that time. Indeed, the laws of the Torah basically differed from their laws. It prohibited worship of idols, which all other peoples then practiced, and substituted the belief in one unseeable God, Creator of the world. The value of human life, then everywhere disregarded, was proclaimed sacred by the Torah, because man was created in the image of God. Respect and consideration were commanded for strangers and foreigners. The Sabbath was instituted, which taught that every seventh day was holy and was to be devoted to rest and to spiritual pursuits. The Torah also contains detailed regulations regarding the government of the people and the duties of the individual toward God, toward the government, and toward mankind. The Torah thus became

155

the Law and the strength of the Jews. Armed with it, they ascended the stage of history, where they played an outstanding and unique role.

The Judges

The Land of Canaan had long been divinely promised to the Jewish people. After they had wandered in the Sinai Desert for forty years, the Jews entered Canaan under the leadership of Joshua, Moses' disciple. But occupation of the country was not an easy matter. Nearly two hundred years elapsed before it became theirs. During this time the Jews engaged in many struggles. Canaan had strong fortified cities that had to be conquered. Before these were taken, the Jewish tribes were separated from one another. This gave rise to the institution of "Judges." Each tribe lived under the leadership of a Judge whom they obeyed, and who led them in war against their enemies. There were many great leaders among them, but not one succeeded in unifying all the tribes into a single government.

During this time the Jews also found it difficult to resist the influence of their Canaanite neighbors. Though they possessed a great spiritual treasure in the Torah, their material civilization was poor, because they had but recently emerged from a state of slavery. The Canaanites, on the other hand, were a wealthy people living in well-built cities and enjoying the comforts of civilization. Many Jews fell under the spell of this civilization and forgot the teachings of the Torah. When admonished by their leaders, they would return temporarily to the ways of God as taught in the Torah, but they frequently slipped back.

The Prophetess Deborah, and her military leader Barak, largely completed the conquest of the country. Unification of the nation was nearly achieved. A central sanctuary was established in Shiloh. But there still existed no central government. The Judges still ruled over single tribes, or groups of tribes.

The Rise of the Kingdom

Samuel, last of the Judges and priest-prophet, yielded to the demands of the people that a king be appointed to rule them. He did so reluctantly, pointing out the disadvantages of an all-powerful monarch. But when the people insisted, he anointed Saul as the first king over Israel. Saul ruled for twenty years. He was successful in many of his wars against the Philistines, but his reign ended tragically. This was due to a number of causes. Saul disobeyed the commands of God as voiced by Samuel. He also became jealous of the young hero David, who had distinguished himself when he slew the Philistine champion Goliath. Irked by David's rising popularity, Saul became mentally ill. Because of the king's growing jealousy, David was forced to flee and gather a following of his own. These events diminished Saul's power, and together with his son Jonathan he was killed in a battle against the Philistines.

After a brief interregnum, David became king. Though marked by a number of rebellions, his reign was glorious. He decisively defeated the Philistines; he took the last unconquered fortress of the Jebusites and established there the city of

Jerusalem, which became the eternal capital of Israel. He extended his conquests far and wide.

The personality of David became a model for all future Jewish rulers. Though subject to sudden passions, David's repentance was so profound and sincere that a prophet assured eternity to David's dynasty. Deeply pious, David expressed his feelings in the world's most beautiful hymns, which are included in the Book of Psalms. David wanted to use the great wealth he acquired for construction of a Temple, but he was told that he could not build it, because he had shed too much blood. Instead the Temple would be built by his son, Solomon, a king of peace.

During Solomon's reign the glory of the kingdom reached its height. He preserved the empire his father had built, by means of efficient administration and alliances with neighboring states. These policies brought him peace. Solomon made Israel a prosperous commercial center. With the help of Hiram, king of Tyre, he sent fleets of ships to distant lands to transport gold and precious stones. Much of these riches was used for building the Temple.

Solomon is remembered for his wisdom. He was also a great poet. Three books in the Bible, The Song of Songs, Ecclesiastes, and Proverbs, are said to have been written by him. But Solomon's rule was also marred by injudicious acts which led to tragedy. His marriages to foreign princesses brought on a partial revival of idolatry, and the heavy taxes he levied to maintain the splendor of his court aroused much dissatisfaction, especially in the northern part of the kingdom.

The Kingdom Divided in Two

When Solomon died, the northern ten tribes broke away and set up a separate kingdom called Israel. The tribes of Judah and Benjamin remained loyal to Solomon's son, who ruled over the kingdom of Judah. This political division was not the only rift among the people. The division of Solomon's kingdom was also accompanied by a spiritual breach. In order to dissuade the people of Israel from visiting the Temple in Jerusalem, the king of Israel, Jeroboam, set up two sanctuaries in his own realm. These were originally intended for the worship of God, but gradually this was contaminated by the introduction of idols, leading to a revival of idolatry throughout Israel. From this time on, life in Israel presented a continuous struggle between the prophets representing true religion, and the princes and kings who constantly lapsed into idolatry.

Nor was the political life of Israel a happy one. The rebellion against Solomon's son set an example for ambitious men later, and revolts were a frequent occurrence, each bringing to the throne a new dynasty. Still, during the two hundred years of the kingdom of Israel, there were also considerable periods of peace and prosperity.

Far to the northeast of Israel and Judah the Assyrian Empire began to expand. It subjected all small nations in its way. For a time Israel submitted, but when, relying on aid from Egypt, King Hosea ben Ela rebelled, the Assyrians besieged Samaria, capital of Israel, and captured it three years later. True to the policy of the Assyrian conquerors, Sargon exiled a part of the people to a distant land, and in their place settled folk from other lands. These people adopted some of the precepts of Judaism. They became known as "Samaritans." A handful remain to this day in the city of Schechem, now known as Nablus.

The Kingdom of Judah

The kingdom of Judah existed much longer. There was one Davidic dynasty and the majority of the kings followed true Judaism. Assyria also came into Judah and subjected it for a time. King Hezekiah rebelled, relying on Egypt's promises. The Assyrian king, Sennacherib, besieged Jerusalem, but the city was miraculously saved when the Assyrian army, stricken by plague, was forced to retire. That ended Assyria's rule. The reigns of Hezekiah and Jehoash were periods of great religious revival. After Assyria, Babylonia came into Judah, and for a short time, King Jehoiakim submitted to these masters. But soon he too rebelled and the Babylonians besieged Jerusalem and exiled his son, Jehoiachin, and part of the people. Zedekiah then became king; when he revolted, the siege was renewed. Jerusalem fell — 586 B.C.E. The Temple was burned and the people were exiled.

The Prophets

The period of the kings was distinguished by the activity of the prophets. Prophecy became a factor in Jewish life at the time of Samuel, but its effects grew more pronounced after Elijah. Inspired by the divine spirit, all the prophets fought against idolatry and insisted on ethical conduct. They feared no one and chastised the rich and the powerful for their wrongdoing. So great was their moral authority that even powerful kings like Ahab trembled before their wrath. Amos emphasized the universality of God. Isaiah foretold the spread of knowledge of God throughout the world, and the reign of peace on earth when "nation shall not lift up sword against nation." Jeremiah taught the eternity of the Jewish people. All the prophets told of a bright future, "in the end of days," the days of the Messiah. The words of the prophets are a great spiritual and moral heritage not only for the Jewish people, but for all humanity.

The Second Commonwealth

The exile of the Jews in Babylonia lasted only forty-seven years — a short time, when compared with the later Jewish dispersion. But its effects on Jewish history were great. Surprisingly, it was in their Babylonian exile that the Jews once and for all renounced all pagan beliefs and practices, and became unwavering believers in pure monotheism.

SILVER SHEKEL OF THE FIRST REVOLT (66-70 C.E.)
Obverse: Chalice with knob on stem. Inscription: Shekel of Israel, Year 3.
Reverse: Stem with bunch of three pomegranates. Inscription: "Jerusalem the Holy"

As a people they never relapsed again. The Babylonian exile also marked the beginning of the Jewish Diaspora. When Cyrus of Persia, who had conquered Babylonia, permitted the exiles to return, only a small number traveled to Jerusalem with their leader Zerubabel — 42,300 all told. Another thousand returned later with Ezra the scribe. The majority remained in Babylonia and in neighboring countries, without losing their loyalty to Judaism. Those who returned succeeded in rebuilding the Temple in the year 516 B.C.E.

We do not know much about the hundred years that elapsed from the death of Ezra and Nehemiah to the conquest of the country by Alexander the Great. We do know that the Jews enjoyed autonomy in Eretz Israel under Persian suzerainty. They were headed by a governing body called "The Great Assembly," which in turn was headed by the high priest. Much intellectual activity was carried on by a group known as *Soferim* (Scribes), who interpreted the Torah and made it fit the conditions of life at that time. Many laws which had been passed on orally and were known to only a few, were now revealed to all the people. During the era of the Scribes and the Great Assembly, the daily prayers and the public reading of the Law on Sabbaths and other days were instituted.

Independence
The Jews first met the Greeks when Alexander the Great conquered the East. At first Palestine (or Judea) was governed by the Greek rulers of Egypt. Later the Greek kings of Syria took the country from Egypt. Greek culture was highly developed and the aristocratic families of Jewish society fell under its spell. A process of assimilation set in. When Antiochus Epiphanes ascended the throne of Syria, he undertook to force the Greek way of life upon all Jews. The Temple was desecrated with a statue of Zeus, and Jews were forbidden to practice the most important rites of their religion. This led to a rebellion under the leadership of Mattathias the Hasmonean, a priest of the city of Modin, and his five sons. Judah, most valiant of Mattathias' sons, succeeded in defeating the Greeks and rededicating the Temple in 165 B.C.E. This occasion gave rise to the festival of Chanukah.

The struggle for independence went on for a considerable time. Judah was killed in one of the battles, but his brother Jonathan succeeded in winning autonomy. Simon, another of Mattathias' sons, won full independence and established the Maccabean — or Hasmonean — dynasty which ruled the country for 103 years.

Subjection
This was a time of strength and expansion for the Jewish State, but there was also much internal strife. Various parties appeared on the scene. There were the Sadducees, who consisted largely of aristocrats. The Pharisees, a people's party, broadly interpreted the Torah laws to apply to all details of life. The conflicts between these parties often led to strife and even to civil war. This provided the huge and expanding Roman empire an opportunity to intervene.

The Jewish princelings who contended for the throne brought their dispute before

Pompey, a Roman general. Pompey utilized his position as arbitrator to impose Roman rule. In 63 B.C.E. he entered Jerusalem. For a time, descendants of the Hasmoneans continued to rule under Roman tutelage. Then the Romans made Herod king of Judea. Herod's sympathies were largely with the Romans. His reign was materially prosperous, but he ruled with an iron hand, and committed many crimes, including the murder of his wife Miriam, a descendant of the Hasmoneans, and their two sons. After Herod's death, Judea became a Roman province.

Roman rule in Judea was oppressive, and in 66 C.E. a great rebellion broke out. Not all the Jews were of the same mind concerning the revolt. Some wished to fight for outright independence; others were in favor of making peace with Rome, realizing that it was impossible to defeat the mighty Roman empire.

In 67 the Roman general, Vespasian, undertook to subdue the rebel Jews. His son, Titus, besieged Jerusalem in the spring of 70 C.E. The beleaguered Jews, short of food and water, fought valiantly against the numerous and well-armed Roman legions. They held out for six months. Toward the end of the siege both food and water were completely gone. Still they fought, retreating to a successive series of fortresses when driven from more advanced posts. The Romans had the most modern instruments of siege of that day. The Jews had their faith and their determination. On the ninth day of Av, the part of the city still in Jewish hands fell to the Romans. The Temple was burned and the city was destroyed.

Spiritual and Cultural Life

Throughout this period, there was great spiritual activity. Study of the Torah and Oral Law increasingly became the all-embracing interest of large masses. The government itself was conducted with the help of the Sanhedrin, a parliament of scholars and important laymen. The scholars interpreted the religious, civil, and criminal laws of Judaism. The laymen dealt with political and administrative matters. Most of the members were of the Pharisaic party. The scholarly section was headed by a president and dean. At the time of Herod, there lived the great Hillel, a man of remarkable character. His statement: "That which is hateful unto thyself, do not do unto others," became a cardinal principle of Jewish ethics.

The New Concept of Judaism

The Romans struck a special medal after the conquest of Jerusalem, which read "Judaea Capta" — Judea is captured. True, Judea had been conquered, the State was gone, but the nation was not destroyed. Many Jews remained in Eretz Israel; a large number lived in other lands, in Babylonia, Egypt, and Rome itself. The Torah and Judaism became the fatherland of the Jews, and hope for redemption and faith in the coming of Messiah became strong factors in Jewish survival.

To keep the Jewish people united wherever they were, a spiritual center was necessary, and that center was provided by the great scholar Johanan ben Zakkai, a disciple of Hillel, who left Jerusalem some time before its destruction and established an Academy at Jabneh. There gathered many scholars, who reconstituted the

Sanhedrin, which exercised authority in all religious, civil, and social matters affecting Jews over the world. It standardized the important prayers and made prayer the main form of worship. When Johanan died, the presidency of the Sanhedrin passed to descendants of Hillel.

Soon a new storm broke. The longing of the people for independence could not easily be put down. A rebellion led by Simeon bar Kochba attracted a large number of followers, among them the greatest spiritual leader and scholar of the age, Rabbi Akiba. Within a year, Roman rule was swept out of the country, Jerusalem was recaptured, and a Jewish government established. Rome sent its best general and many legions, and after a bitter struggle of two years the last stronghold, Bethar, fell, and Simeon was killed. The number of Jews slain ran into hundreds of thousands, the cities destroyed into hundreds. Hadrian took cruel revenge. He aimed to wipe out Judaism, and severe punishment was meted out upon all observers, especially those who taught the Torah. Rabbi Akiba challenged the Roman decree and died a martyr while teaching. He thus inspired later generations of Jews to undergo martyrdom for their religion.

When Antoninus Pius revoked Hadrian's decrees in 138 C.E., life became normal again to some extent. The Academy and the Sanhedrin moved to Galilee and continued their activity. But the effects of the rebellion were evident; the population had decreased, poverty prevailed, and emigration to other lands assumed large proportions. It was then that Judah the Prince, head of the Academy, decided to compile a work that would stabilize Judaism all over the world. In collaboration with other scholars, he edited the Mishnah, in six parts. Hitherto, the extensive Jewish law had been orally taught in various schools, and this gave rise to many differences. Now a written text was made available to all scholars.

Eretz Israel and Babylonia

During the next three hundred years there were two centers of world Jewry. There arose the center in Babylonia, where the Jewish population was large, and economic and political conditions were favorable. Learning had been cultivated there before, but it rose to still greater heights when Aba Arika, a student of Judah the Prince, returned with the Mishnah and opened an Academy at Sura. His colleague, Samuel, taught at Nehardea, and Rab Yehudah, a disciple of both, founded the Academy at Pumpbedita (247 C.E.). The heads of the Academies, as well as other outstanding scholars, were called *amoraim*, commentators, for they interpreted the Mishnah.

Similar activity went on in Palestine. Here, too, *amoraim* expounded the Mishnah and elucidated regulations for the Jewish way of life. For a time, these exerted influence upon Jewish settlements in Egypt, Arabia, and the early communities in southern Europe. But soon the political situation worsened. The Roman empire became officially Christian and began to persecute the Jews. For a short time, though, a ray of light broke forth. The Roman emperor, Julian, who is called the apostate, for he preferred paganism to Christianity, favored the Jews and wanted to rebuild the Temple. His plan was not carried out, and he died shortly thereafter in battle (362). The situation under succeeding emperors grew worse, and learning diminished. In the reign of Theodosius II, the Academies were closed.

As the influence of Palestine declined, the Babylonian center gained in importance, especially after the Talmud was compiled. As generations of teachers continued to expound the law, it became necessary to collect and write down all the accepted interpretations and discussions. This work — the Talmud — was a complished in 352-427 C.E. by a group of scholars under the guidance of Rab Ashi.

The Talmud includes the Mishnah plus all the comments and explanations of generations of scholars. The comments are called Gemara. It contains not only laws for regulating Jewish social life, but also ethical teachings, historical information, and stories about the deeds of great men of all generations. The Talmud is divided into sixty-three tractates, each dealing with a separate subject. It was finished in the year 500 C.E. and became Jewry's primary literature supplementing the Bible.

The Period of the Geonim

The post-talmudic period, 500-1038 C.E., is marked by important events in Jewish history. For several centuries, Babylonia remained a center of influence in world Jewry. The heads of the two Babylonian academies, called *geonim,* after the Talmud was compiled, continued to guide many communities in Asia and in Europe. But, many changes entered into the life of Babylonian Jewry through the emergence of a new religion and a new political power. This religion is known as Mohammedanism, or Islam. After the death of its founder, Mohammed (632 C.E.), the new faith was spread by force of arms over much of Asia, part of Africa, and Spain in Europe. The Jews of Palestine, Egypt, Babylonia, and all other parts of the Persian empire came under Moslem rule. The language of the conquerors was Arabic, and they developed an extensive culture in Babylonia and many other countries.

This new turn of events radically changed Jewish life. Arabic became the spoken language of the Jews, though they did not forget Hebrew and continued to cherish it. They also began to develop a rich literature of Bible commentaries, Hebrew grammar, and philosophy. In this field the work of Saadia Gaon (892-942 C.E.) is most distinguished. A great part of the literature was composed in Arabic, or Judaeo-Arabic, but many works were also written in Hebrew.

About the middle of the eighth century, a man named Anan founded a sect which claimed literal obedience to the Bible and rejected the Talmud — or the Oral Law. His followers called themselves Karaites, from the Hebrew word *mikra* — the Scriptures. The sect spread through other countries, but won over only a fraction of the Jews. A small number still exist today.

Two medieval Jewish kingdoms were founded by gentile converts in both the Arabic and Christian worlds. One, in Arabia of the pre-Islamic period, lasted about thirty years. Its last king, Joseph Dhu Nuwas, died 525 C.E. in a war with the Christians of Ethiopia. The other was the kingdom of the Khazars, a Mongolian people who lived in the steppes of the Volga. They were converted to Judaism about 740 C.E. and their kingdom lasted for some centuries, until it was overrun by the Russians.

Toward the end of this period, Jewish settlements in Spain, Italy, France, and Germany began to take ascendancy in Jewish life. The Babylonian center gradually lost its prestige, and its population began to diminish. The Academies were closed (1038 C.E.) and the office of the Gaon ceased to exist.

The Middle Ages

For Jews, the Middle Ages occupy the the span of time from 1000 C.E. to 1750 C.E. This period marked the rise of Jewish centers in Europe, first in southern and western Europe, and later in eastern Europe. With few exceptions, this was a time of great physical suffering, but also of vast intellectual activity, resulting in an extensive literature.

Throughout Europe, the Jews had few rights, and were barely tolerated by kings, princes, and feudal lords. Expulsions from cities and countries are too numerous to be listed here; the same holds true for assaults and massacres. But one must mention the First Crusade and the religious fanaticism and Jew-hatred it created. In 1096, the Jews in northern France and Germany were attacked and massacred by the Crusaders. The number of the slain is estimated as 12,000 — at least one third of the Jews in Germany. This was followed by the Second (1146), Third (1187), and Fourth (1202 — 4) Crusades, during which Jews were everywhere massacred. In 1290, the Jews were expelled from England, and in 1394 from France. When the Black Death spread through Europe (1348-50) and killed twenty-five million people, Jews, falsely accused of poisoning the wells, were again brutally massacred. In 1391, the people of Spain, excited by fanatics, attacked the Jews, half of whom were either killed or forcibly converted. This marks the beginning of the *Marrano-Jews* who outwardly professed Christianity while secretly observing Judaism. The year 1492 saw the expulsion of all the Jews from Spain (about 200,000). Many died from starvation or disease and a number settled in North Africa, Turkey, Palestine, and several European countries. A century later, in 1593, Marrano Jews also settled in Holland.

Cossack Massacres

The large settlement of Jews in Poland suffered disaster in the years 1648-50, when the Cossacks, under Chmielnicki, rebelled against the Poles, and destroyed many Jewish communities on the assumption that Jews were too friendly to the Poles. It is estimated that a quarter of a million Jews perished. The miracle of Jewish survival, under such circumstances, is to be explained by steadfast devotion to religion and ideals, and by strong belief in the coming redemption and the return to the Holy Land, as promised by the prophets.

Cultural Flowering

In those countries where Jews were better treated, they took part in the general life and developed their own culture to a high degree. The years from 1000 to 1200 in Spain, we call the Golden Age. Solomon ibn Gabirol (1021-1058), Bachya ibn Pakuda (fl. 1050), and Judah ha-Levi (1085-1142) wrote philosophical books in Arabic, and Judah Halevi's magnificent poems won him the title of sweet singer of Zion. Abraham ibn Ezra (1093-1167) wrote excellent commentaries on the Bible, books on astronomy, and Hebrew poems. Maimonides (Moses ben Maimon, born in Spain 1135, died in Egypt 1204), greatest of medieval Jews, composed outstanding books on medicine; a great philosophic work "Guide For the Perplexed" in Judaeo-Arabic; and a comprehensive code of Jewish law (Mishneh Torah) in Hebrew.

Among Jews of France and Germany, the intellectual activity was carried on in Hebrew, consisting in study of the Bible, the Talmud, and rabbinic law. Translations from Judaeo-Arabic into Hebrew had been made of the great Jewish works. There was Rabbi Gershom, "Light of the Exile" (960-1040), among whose many ordinances were those promulgating monogamy and regulating divorce. Here, too, lived Solomon ben Isaac (1040-1105), known as *Rashi,* whose commentaries on the Bible and the Talmud clarified the texts and made them readily available to students to this very day. Joseph Karo of Spain (1488-1575), who settled in Palestine after the expulsion, compiled a complete code of Jewish law called *Shulhan Arukh,* which is still the standard for traditional Judaism.

False Messiahs

Whenever great suffering occurred, messianic movements arose. The period from 1492 to the end of the 18th century produced a number of such movements. The most important was that of Sabbetai Zevi (1620-1676) which originated in Smyrna (Turkey) and attracted followers among Jews everywhere. It ended disastrously, when the leader, seized by the Turks, accepted Islam. He died a prisoner in an Albanian fortress. In 1759, another movement arose in southern Poland, headed by Jacob Frank. It, too, attracted many followers and ended similarly by the conversion of Frank and his disciples to Catholicism.

Hassidism

In the eighteenth century a new and powerful movement arose among Jews in eastern Europe. This was *Hassidism.* The founder of the movement was Rabbi Israel Baal Shem Tov — "Master of the Good Name" (1700-1759). The basic principle of this movement was that piety and love of God were fully as important as scholarly disputation. As a result of this principle, *hassidim* ascribed as great worth to fervent prayer as to study of talmudic law. Hassidism spread rapidly because it appealed to the poor masses of Jews, many of whom lacked the time for scholarly pursuits.

The successors of Israel Baal Shem Tov gained wide followings, and hassidic congregations soon arose in hundreds of towns. These were like great brotherhoods. The members were devoted to one another.

The hassidic rabbis came to be known as *Zaddikim* (from the Hebrew word for "righteous"). Many of these were truly great men, and their ethical teachings have influenced Jewish life and literature to this day. But some of their followers tended to become too dependent on their rabbis, and to look upon them as miracle workers. Most of the Jews, called *mitnagdim* (opponents), feared that the new movement might undermine study and observance by too great stress on mere emotion. The mitnagdim were also displeased by the great reverence which the hassidim accorded their rabbis. They feared that unless this trend was checked, it might lead to worship of their rabbis as "saints," a principle that is alien to Judaism. The altercations between *hassidim* and *mitnagdim* resulted in much bitterness. Eventually these two major trends in Judaism became reconciled, and the *hassidim* with their appreciation of "the wonder of Jewish life" richly complemented the *mitnagdim* with their strict adherence to "the law of Jewish life." Similarly, the opponents encouraged the *hassidim* to greater interest in study.

The End of the Ghetto (1750-1880)

By the middle of the eighteenth century, the ideas of liberty, equality, and fraternity prevalent in Europe also began to penetrate the Jewish communities of western Europe, and aroused a desire to adjust to the new conditions. This movement was spurred by Moses Mendelssohn (1729-1786), a Jewish philosopher and distinguished writer in the German language. Under his influence Jews began to participate in German culture. This latter movement was called *Haskalah,* which means Enlightenment. It sought to arouse a greater interest in secular learning — literature, science, and art.

The revolution which swept France at the end of the eighteenth century aroused in the Jews a desire to obtain equal rights. For a short time during the reign of Napoleon, the Jews of Germany enjoyed such rights, and this taste of freedom prompted them to introduce changes in their own Jewish modes, to resemble those of their neighbors. This desire was the basis of the "Reform" movement, which denied that Jews were a nation, and declared that the Jews of Germany were simply Germans practicing the Mosaic religion.

Persecution in Russia

The struggle for equal rights for Jews met with considerable success in western Europe, but in the east the situation was different. Most Jews of Poland became subjects of the Russian Empire when Poland was largely annexed by Russia. The Russian rulers were hostile toward the Jews. The people were permitted to live only in a small section of Russia known as the Pale of Settlement. During the reign of Nicholas I (1825-1855) young Jewish boys were pressed into military service for twenty-five years. Except for a brief interlude during the reign of Alexander II, the Jews of Russia were constantly oppressed and persecuted.

Creative Cultural Life

But even though they had to suffer great hardships, the Jews of Russia led a creative religious life. Learning flourished and many *yeshivot* (talmudic academies) were established. The *Haskalah* movement gained ground and brought about a true renaissance of Hebrew literature. Many Hebrew newspapers and magazines were founded and prospered. Outstanding Hebrew novelists, like Abraham Mapu (1805-

1867) and Peretz Smolenskin (1842-1885), and gifted poets like Micah Joseph Lebensohn (1828-1852) and Judah Leib Gordon (1831-1892) appeared on the scene.

Emigration

Toward the end of the nineteenth century profound events occurred in Jewish life in Europe. Anti-Semitism became prevalent in western Europe, especially in Germany. In Russia hatred of the Jews assumed the form of physical violence, and many pogroms, in which Jews were murdered and robbed, took place in the early eighteen-eighties.

The pogroms and the new repressions that followed reawakened the Jews of Russia to an appreciation of their true situation. Many who had believed that modern civilization would bring them freedom and equal rights, now realized that their situation was hopeless, and that they would always remain scapegoats. This gave rise to two social movements. One was emigration — flight from Russia. This mass migration was directed largely to the United States, though smaller numbers also went to England and South Africa.

The second movement maintained that security and freedom for Jews to live as Jews could be assured only in the Jewish Homeland. This movement was largely influenced by Leo Pinsker (1821-1891), M.L. Lilienblum (1843-1910), and Rabbi Samuel Mohilever (1824-1898). Small groups called *Hoveve Zion* (Lovers of Zion) were organized, and a number of young men traveled to Palestine to establish agricultural settlements.

Zionism

In 1896, Dr. Theodor Herzl, a Jewish journalist from Vienna, came to Paris to report the trial of Captain Dreyfus. The Dreyfus case, which aroused the interest of the entire world, involved a Jewish officer in the French army falsely accused of treason and sentenced to a long term of imprisonment. (He was ultimately exonerated.) While Dreyfus was on trial, the case was used to fan anti-Jewish hatred. Dr. Herzl became convinced that the only solution to the Jewish problem was the establishment of a Jewish State where Jews could govern themselves. He wrote a book called *Judenstaat* (Jewish State) in which he presented his views. This created a tremendous stir. In 1897, Herzl convoked the first World Zionist Congress, in which Jews from all countries participated. The Congress founded the World Zionist Organization. Herzl conducted negotiations with the Sultan of Turkey (then ruler of Palestine) to obtain the rights to an autonomous settlement of Jews in Palestine. He also visited the rulers of many countries in an effort to win their support for Zionism. Herzl's negotiations were not successful, but many Jews recognized him as their spokesman.

After Herzl died in 1904, the movement continued its work. Many settlements were established in Palestine. Following the 1905 pogroms in Russia, emigration to Palestine gained much momentum. The Zionist movement also conducted extensive educational work. In Palestine, Eliezer ben Yehudah (1858-1922) undertook to make Hebrew the spoken language of the people. His efforts were successfully continued by others. Today Hebrew is the language of the Jews in Israel, and is studied wherever Jews live in freedom.

Two World Wars

In 1914 the First World War broke out. Jews suffered heavily, because so many of them lived in Poland and Russia, where many great battles were fought. When the war ended, Poland was again set up as an independent country, but the Jews of Russia were cut off from the rest of the world as a result of the Bolshevik Revolution. For a short period in 1918, that part of southern Russia known as the Ukraine was independent, and hundreds of thousands of Jews were massacred there.

When the world finally regained some semblance of normalcy after World War I, the Jewish people in eastern Europe found themselves in a sad state. Perhaps the only positive outcome of this war for the Jews, was the issuance of the Balfour Declaration (1917), wherein the British government undertook to make Palestine again the Jewish National Home. The other countries of the world followed suit. The Zionist movement expanded greatly and much work was done in Palestine. Great stretches of desert and swamp land were reclaimed. Cities and villages were established. Scholarship was fostered and a variety of institutions of higher learning were established.

Catastrophe in Europe

But the years of relative peace did not last long. The Jews of Poland, Romania, and Hungary were made to suffer increasing persecution, and a new enemy, more terrible than any before, appeared on the horizon.

In Germany an obscure former corporal named Hitler incited the people against the Jews and gained a great following. His popularity grew so rapidly that by 1933 he became Premier of Germany, and his party, the Nazis, ruled the country. He at once instituted the most terrible dictatorship in history. All the people were denied freedom, but his chief hatred was directed against the Jews of the world.

The Second World War broke out in 1939 when Germany invaded Poland. Within a short time Hitler's armies occupied nearly all of Europe. The greatest crime in history was then committed by the Germans. Millions of Jews were gassed by the Germans in specially constructed "extermination centers." Others were tortured to death. Children and infants were not spared.

By the time World War II ended, six million Jews of Europe — more than one-third of all the Jews in the world — had been slaughtered by the Germans under Hitler.

The one and one-half million Jews who survived in Europe found themselves in horrendous predicament. Most had lost their families. They did not wish to return to their native towns. Temporarily they stayed in what were called "Displaced Persons' Camps." They wanted to migrate to Palestine, but the Arabs opposed their admission and the British rulers of Palestine admitted only an insignificant number.

The Jews of Palestine came to their aid, and thousands of surviving European Jews were brought into the land contrary to the wishes of both British and Arabs. Most of the people in the world sympathized with the plight of the Jews. In November, 1947, the United Nations adopted a resolution approving the division of Palestine into two independent countries, one Jewish and the other Arab.

*   *   *

In April, 1948, the Jews of Palestine proclaimed their independence and opened the gates of their little country, which they named "Israel," to all Jews who wished to come there. The United States first, and many other nations, recognized the new republic. But at once all the Arab countries attacked Israel. It was an uneven struggle; the Jews were outnumbered forty to one. The United Nations failed to come to the aid of Israel. The situation seemed desperate. But the Jews of Israel fought with their backs to the wall, and triumphed over the huge Arab armies.

Since then about thirteen hundred thousand Jews from Europe, Asia, and Africa have entered Israel. Great efforts are being made to reclaim the desert lands to provide food for the immigrants, and many industries have been established. The Jews of America extended, and continue to extend, generous financial and moral aid.

All this time, however, Israel had to be on constant guard against threats to her survival. The Arab countries had not made peace with her. For years, her borders were subjected to raids from Arab infiltrators based in Egypt, particularly in the Gaza Strip. On October 29, 1956, Israel struck back, conquering the Gaza Strip and the Sinai Peninsula in a swift operation that lasted just four days. Captured documents and arms supplies revealed that the Gaza Strip had been readied as a springboard for an Egyptian invasion of Israel. But several months later Israel withdrew her troops from the Gaza Strip and and the Sinai Peninsula at the request of the United Nations.

Beginning late in 1966 Israel's border settlements were increasingly harassed by raids from Arab infiltrators based in Jordan and Syria. In the Spring of 1967 Egypt, Jordan and Syria mobilized for an all-out Arab attack against Israel. After getting the United Nations to withdraw the peace-keeping forces that had been stationed in the Sinai Peninsula and in the Gaza Strip since the war of 1956, and signing a mutual defense pact with Jordan, Egypt's President Abdel Gamel Nasser blockaded the port of Elath, Israel's outlet to the Gulf of Aqaba and the Red Sea.

In the morning of June 5, 1967, Israel retaliated, destroying most of the Arab air force on the ground within hours. With the skies clear of enemy planes, Israel's army was able to move ahead swiftly, occupying the Gaza Strip and the Sinai Peninsula, and reaching the eastern bank of the Suez Canal within eighty-nine hours. When Jordan opened fire on the Israeli sector of Jerusalem, Israel's troops thrust deep into Jordan, occupying the Jordanian sector west of the River Jordan. After three days of fighting, the Old City of Jerusalem was in Israeli hands, and, for the first time in two thousand years, the Wailing Wall was under Jewish control.

Israel next sent her troops into Syria and captured Syrian fortifications in the Golan hills from which the Syrians had been shelling Israeli settlements in the Galilee.

The outbreak of this war set off unprecedented demonstrations of solidarity from world Jewry. Millions of dollars were raised within hours to aid the Israeli war effort, and hundreds of Jews from all over the western world volunteered their services to Israel. But before these volunteers could arrive in Israel in large numbers the fighting was all but over. The entire war had lasted only six days.

WORLD JEWRY TODAY

At the present time there exist only two large Jewish centers in the world — one in the English speaking countries, and the other in Israel. The third large community, in Russia, is cut off from all contact with the rest of the world by an impenetrable curtain, and is being subjected to a policy of religious and cultural obliteration. Smaller but significant Jewish communities exist in some of the Latin American countries. The Jewish communities in Arab lands have greatly decreased in population. Algeria, for instance, which had 120,000 Jews in 1961, now has no more than 2,000.

A continued close relationship between the Jews of Israel and those living in the rest of the free world should hold out much promise for the spiritual and cultural growth and enrichment of the Jewish people as a whole.

HIGHLIGHTS OF AMERICAN JEWISH HISTORY

The Discovery and Settlement of America

When Columbus set out in 1492 to find a short route to India, and discovered America instead, there were Marranos Jews secreted among the crews of his vessels. Jewish history in America thus begins with the history of America itself. Jews were among the first settlers in the New World.

It is recorded that secret synagogues existed in the New World in the 1500's. In 1630 the Netherlands occupied part of Brazil, and the Marranos living there openly returned to Judaism. About two thousand Jews from Europe also emigrated there, and the first free Jewish congregation in the New World was established in the city of Recife.

But the rule of the Netherlands did not last long. In 1654 the Portuguese drove the Dutch out of Brazil, and the Jews were forced to leave. Some went back to the home country, some to other Dutch colonies in America. A small group of twenty-three Jews sailed northward and reached New Amsterdam (now New York) in September, 1654.

The First Jewish Community in North America

Though individual Jews had lived in North America before 1654, those who came from Brazil constituted the first permanent Jewish settlement. At first the governor of New Amsterdam, Peter Stuyvesant, refused to let them stay. They appealed to the Dutch West India Company, in whose behalf Stuyvesant governed, and obtained a Grant of Privileges to live and trade there. Within two years they also obtained the rights to travel, to own houses, to maintain a cemetery, and other privileges. But though they held services in homes, they were not granted the right to establish a synagogue. It was only in 1664, when New Amsterdam was annexed by England and renamed New York, that a declaration of religious freedom was issued, giving them the right to rent a house of worship for their congregation, which was named *Shearith Israel.*

The Spread of Jewish Settlement

Other Jewish communities soon came into existence. In 1658, fifteen Jewish families settled in Newport, Rhode Island. Jews came to Connecticut in 1659; to North Carolina in 1665; to Georgia in 1733.

Jewish immigration continued throughout the colonial period. It originated in England, Holland, Germany, Poland. The immigrants were traders, artisans, physicians. Wherever ten Jewish men (the quorum required for public worship, called a *minyan*) settled, they met to worship. They established cemeteries, and formed congregations. When their numbers increased, they built synagogues. In 1727, the congregation *Shearith Israel* built its first synagogue on Mill street.

Most of these early American Jews were Sefardim (decended from the Jews of Spain and Portugal). They clung devoutly to their faith, but did not segregate themselves socially, nor did their Christian neighbors shun them in any manner. The groundwork for the free American society that emerged later, was already being laid, and these early Jews actively participated in this society. They formed partnerships with their neighbors. There were Jewish students at the University of Pennsylvania in the 1760's. Jews accompanied George Washington in his expedition against the French. Ezra Stiles, President of Yale University, sought the company of Jewish scholars. He also studied Hebrew and visited the synagogue at Newport.

Hebrew Influence on Early America

Integration of the early Jews into the new American society was facilitated by a number of factors. The spirit of religious equality was strong in the land, because the country was being settled by various sects and denominations. The Puritans were deeply devoted to the Bible, and their ministers studied Hebrew. The Hebraic influence was so great, in fact, that at one time it was suggested that Hebrew be made the official language of the country.

The Revolutionary War

It was natural that the Jews should participate actively in the Revolutionary War that won independence for the United States. There were only about 2,000 Jews in the thirteen colonies at the time. Many Jews fought under Washington. Jewish merchants helped to raise funds to finance the war. The best known of these was Haym Salomon. George Washington took cognizance of Jewish aid in the cause of American independence, in letters of praise to various congregations.

Immigration from Central Europe

Jews from Central Europe came to America throughout the colonial period. At the time of the Revolution, these Jews, called Ashkenazim, already outnumbered the Sephardic Jews.

After 1815, when severe repressions set in, in Europe, German-speaking Jews began to arrive in ever increasing numbers. Of 6,000 Jews in the United States in 1826, more than three-quarters were Germans. In 1848 Central Europe experienced great political unrest which led to another tide of German-Jewish immigration. Many of these newcomers settled in the Middle West and Far West. At first they faced a hard struggle for existence. But soon they attained economic well-being, and contributed greatly to development of the frontier settlements. As traders, merchants, and artisans, they brought to outlying communities the comforts of civilization and higher standards of living.

The German-speaking Jews also developed an active Jewish life outside the synagogue. They established fraternal and literary societies, founding *Bnai Brith* with twelve members in 1843. Within a short time this order had thousands of members. Today it numbers hundreds of thousands. Other fraternal and benevolent organizations, such as the *Brith Abraham,* developed rapidly.

The German immigrants also established many congregations and synagogues. In 1825 they had only two; by 1848 there were seventy-seven synagogues throughout the country. Some also maintained Hebrew Schools for the children. However, many of the small communities lacked qualified teachers.

The Civil War

At the time of the Civil War, the Jewish population of the United States numbered nearly 200,000. Jews were active in national life. They participated in John Brown's revolt against slavery. They were among the founders of the Republican Party. Some also took a leading part on the side of the South. (Judah P. Banjamin was Secretary of State of the Confederate States.) About 6,000 Jews served in the Union ranks; another 1,200 wore the uniform of the Confederacy.

Rise of the Reform Movement

The period from 1850 to 1880 marked the peak of German Jewish immigration.

It is estimated that about 100,000 German Jews entered this country during that time.

This period also marked the rise of Reform Judaism in the United States. Most of the new arrivals were saturated with the spirit of religious change. With them came a number of rabbis who had been leaders of the movement in Germany. Outstanding among these was Isaac Meyer Wise (1819-1900). Rabbi Wise organized the Union of American Hebrew Congregations in 1873. He also founded in 1875 the *Hebrew Union College* at Cincinnati to train rabbis. The latter institution is now merged with the *Jewish Institute of Religion,* which was founded by Dr. Stephen S. Wise in 1922.

Achievements of German Jewish Immigrants

The German Jewish immigration, which shaped Jewish life in America through most of the nineteenth century, has many notable achievements to its credit. It built many charitable institutions, including the famed Mt. Sinai Hospital in New York. In 1859 the United Hebrew Charities was established. It organized large and influential fraternal and social orders. A thriving periodical press was established in both the German and English languages. At this time, too, American Jews began to take an active interest in the defense of persecuted Jewish communities abroad, as in the case of the blood libel against the Jews of Damascus, and persecutions in Switzerland and in the Papal States. Economic relief activities in Palestine were also undertaken.

Mordecai Emanuel Noah (1785-1851)

Mordecai Emanuel Noah, a distinguished journalist, active in this country's political life (he served as American consul in Tunis for several years), dreamed the age-old hope of the Jewish people: to overcome dispersion and oppression. In 1825 he undertook the ambitious project of establishing a Jewish state on Grand Island in the Niagara River, near the Falls. He bought the land, then still a wilderness, and wrote to Jewish communities in Europe to come make their home there. Inauguration of his project was celebrated in a church in Buffalo, New York, on September 2, 1825 He hoped that in time the small project on Grand Island might expand into the surrounding unsettled countryside, and provide a haven of safety for the Jews of Europe. But his appeals remained unanswered.

The New Immigration from Eastern Europe

In 1881-1882, and again in 1905, waves of bloody pogroms swept the Jewish

HEBREW UNION COLLEGE, CINCINNATI, OHIO — REFORM

communities in Czarist Russia. This persecution gave rise to the vast Jewish migration from East Europe. There were only about 250,000 Jews in the United States in 1880. By the time this mass immigration was virtually halted as a result of racist laws in 1924, the Jewish community had grown to four and a half million.

These newcomers, Yiddish-speaking, faced difficult conditions. They worked in factories, where they had to labor long hours for meager wages. Conditions in these establishments were so bad that they came to be known as "sweatshops." Economically poor, and forlorn in their new environment, the immigrants crowded into slums.

However, they enjoyed some important advantages. They brought with them a rich cultural heritage of learning and tradition. They were self-reliant, had a keen sense of responsibility for Jews overseas, and a strong feeling for social justice. They cherished a great love for America, which had given them freedom and opportunity after the persecutions suffered in Eastern Europe.

The Eastern Jews established schools and academies. They organized self-help institutions, labor and fraternal orders and *Landsmannschaften* (organizations of persons from the same town in the Old Country).

Many political educational and social movements aiming to improve the lot of Jews, and of humanity in general, grew popular. Zionism, socialism, and other nationalist and political trends had wide followings in the crowded immigrant districts. They also organized themselves into labor unions to fight for better working conditions. Within a relatively short time they achieved many of their economic goals, and the sweatshops became a thing of the past.

The Yiddish Press and Literature

Unlike the Jewish immigrants of the eighteenth and early nineteenth centuries, those who came from Eastern Europe clung to the Yiddish language. The first Yiddish weekly magazine appeared in 1885. Later a number of Yiddish dailies were established. The most influential of these, The *Jewish Daily Forward,* and *The Day — Jewish Morning Journal,* have a large number of readers to this day. These periodicals helped the immigrants in many ways. The Yiddish press helped preserve the cultural values the immigrants had brought with them; it imparted American culture and ways of life, and led them to higher standards of living.

In addition to newspapers and magazines, an extensive literature in Yiddish was produced in the United States. Poets, novelists, story writers, and dramatists produced important works, many of which were to be translated into English.

The Hebrew Press and Literature

A Hebrew press and literature also developed, though on a smaller scale than Yiddish. At one time a Hebrew daily was published in New York. Since Hebrew was not the spoken language of the masses, its use was largely restricted to literature, education, and religion. At present Hebrew is gaining in popularity, with numerous Hebrew schools and the introduction of the study into many high schools, colleges, and universities. There are also a number of Hebrew periodicals in Amer-

ica. *Hadoar,* now over thirty years old, is the only Hebrew weekly outside Israel.
Relief Agencies.

The Jewish immigrants felt responsibility for the welfare of Jews throughout the world. There evolved organizations and institutions whose chief purpose was to aid needy Jews abroad and recent arrivals in this country. In 1898 *HIAS* (Hebrew Sheltering and Immigrant Aid Society) was founded. For more than fifty years this organization helped thousands of immigrants overcome their difficulties of adjustment to the new circumstances. During World War I, when Jews in Europe suffered great hardship, the American Jewish Joint Distribution Committee (J.D.C.) was established. This organization has been carrying on its work since 1914 in many countries. At this time it is most active in North Africa and Israel. When refugees from German persecution began to arrive in this country, the United Service for New Americans was established to help them during their first years.

Educational Institutions

As the mass of immigrants settled down and began to feel more at home, they devoted themselves to their educational and spiritual needs. *The Jewish Theological Seminary,* which trains rabbis for conservative synagogues, was established in 1886, and it has been expanding its activities ever since. In 1896 the *Rabbi Isaac Elchanan Theological Seminary* was founded in New York to train orthodox rabbis. This institution is now *Yeshiva University,* with graduate, medical, and other colleges.

THE JEWISH THEOLOGICAL SEMINARY OF AMERICA, NEW YORK CITY — CONSERVATIVE